Mastering Reading Skills

2

Mastering Reading Skills Book 2

Publisher Chung Kyudo
Editors Kim Jinsuk, Cho Sangik
Author Michael A. Putlack
Designers Yoon Jiyoung, Park Sunyoung

First published in November 2013
By Darakwon, Inc.
Darakwon Bldg., 211, Munbal-ro, Paju-si, Gyeonggi-do 10881
Republic of Korea
Tel: 82-2-736-2031 (Ext. 250)
Fax: 82-2-732-2037

Price ₩12,000
ISBN 978-89-277-0691-5 54740
978-89-277-0688-5 54740 (set)

www.darakwon.co.kr

Components Main Book / Workbook
11 10 9 8 7 6 5 21 22 23 24 25

Mastering Reading Skills

2

DARAKWON

Table of Contents

Introduction

Mastering Reading Skills Book 2 is the fourth book in a four-book series. This book is intended for intermediate learners of the English language. By using this book, learners will be able to improve their reading skills as well as their knowledge of English.

Mastering Reading Skills Book 2 contains twenty units. The twenty units are divided into five topics, each of which contains four units. The five topics in *Mastering Reading Skills Book 2* are Weather, Literature, Modern Technology, Economics, and Ancient Societies. These are all topics that young learners find interesting and enjoy learning about. So learners will have fun reading the material in this book while improving their English at the same time.

Every unit contains one main passage, a shorter passage, and questions about these passages. Each unit also contains a reading skill and exercises on it. The reading skills will help learners improve various aspects of their reading abilities.

Mastering Reading Skills Book 2 has several objectives. First, it will help learners improve their English abilities, particularly their reading skills. Next, it will teach them valuable knowledge about a wide range of academic topics. The passages themselves will also entertain learners as they read. Finally, *Mastering Reading Skills Book 2* will help learners prepare for various standardized tests that they may take in the future. For instance, many questions about the passages are similar to those that appear on the iBT TOEFL® Junior and iBT TOEFL® exams. So, by using this book, learners should be able to get higher scores on the tests they take in the future.

About This Book

There are a total of twenty units. Each unit contains one main passage about a specific topic. There are vocabulary and reading comprehension questions about the main passage. There is also a shorter passage with reading comprehension questions. There are a total of ten reading skills that are taught in the various chapters. Finally, there is a comprehensive vocabulary section as well as a workbook that will help learners increase their understanding of the passages and improve their English abilities.

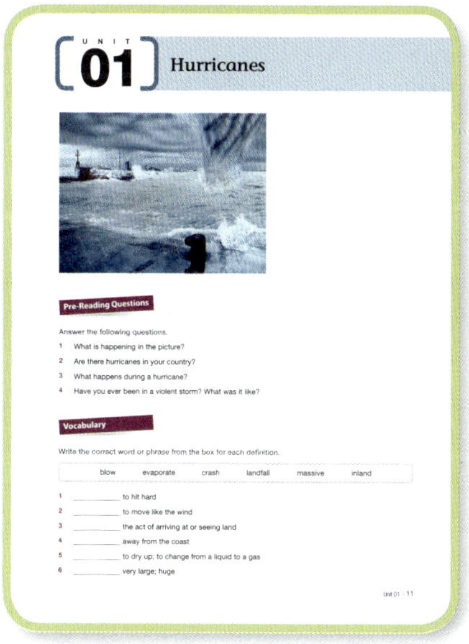

UNIT 01 Hurricanes

Pre-Reading Questions

Answer the following questions.

1 What is happening in the picture?
2 Are there hurricanes in your country?
3 What happens during a hurricane?
4 Have you ever been in a violent storm? What was it like?

Vocabulary

Write the correct word or phrase from the box for each definition.

blow evaporate crash landfall massive inland

1 ______ to hit hard
2 ______ to move like the wind
3 ______ the act of arriving at or seeing land
4 ______ away from the coast
5 ______ to dry up; to change from a liquid to a gas
6 ______ very large; huge

Unit 01 · 11

Pre-Reading Questions

There are four questions that focus on the picture or pictures at the top of the page. These questions will help prepare learners for the topic of the unit.

Vocabulary

This section contains six vocabulary words from the main passage. Learners should match the words with the definitions.

Passage

This is the main passage of the unit. Each passage is around 220-250 words long and focuses on the topic of the unit.

Summary

This is a short summary of the unit. There are five blanks for learners to fill in by using words in the box above the summary.

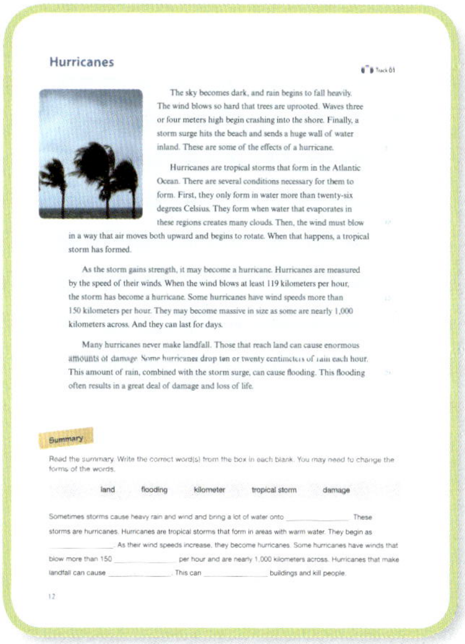

Hurricanes

Track 01

The sky becomes dark, and rain begins to fall heavily. The wind blows so hard that trees are uprooted. Waves three or four meters high begin crashing into the shore. Finally, a storm surge hits the beach and sends a huge wall of water inland. These are some of the effects of a hurricane.

Hurricanes are tropical storms that form in the Atlantic Ocean. There are several conditions necessary for them to form. First, they only form in water more than twenty-six degrees Celsius. They form when water that evaporates in these regions creates many clouds. Then, the wind must blow in a way that air moves both upward and begins to rotate. When that happens, a tropical storm has formed.

As the storm gains strength, it may become a hurricane. Hurricanes are measured by the speed of their winds. When the wind blows at least 119 kilometers per hour, the storm has become a hurricane. Some hurricanes have wind speeds more than 150 kilometers per hour. They may become massive in size as some are nearly 1,000 kilometers across. And they can last for days.

Many hurricanes never make landfall. Those that reach land can cause enormous amounts of damage. Some hurricanes drop ten or twenty centimeters of rain each hour. This amount of rain, combined with the storm surge, can cause flooding. This flooding often results in a great deal of damage and loss of life.

Summary

Read the summary. Write the correct word(s) from the box in each blank. You may need to change the forms of the words.

land flooding kilometer tropical storm damage

Sometimes storms cause heavy rain and wind and bring a lot of water onto ______. These storms are hurricanes. Hurricanes are tropical storms that form in areas with warm water. They begin as ______. As their wind speeds increase, they become hurricanes. Some hurricanes have winds that blow more than 150 ______ per hour and are nearly 1,000 kilometers across. Hurricanes that make landfall can cause ______. This can ______ buildings and kill people.

12

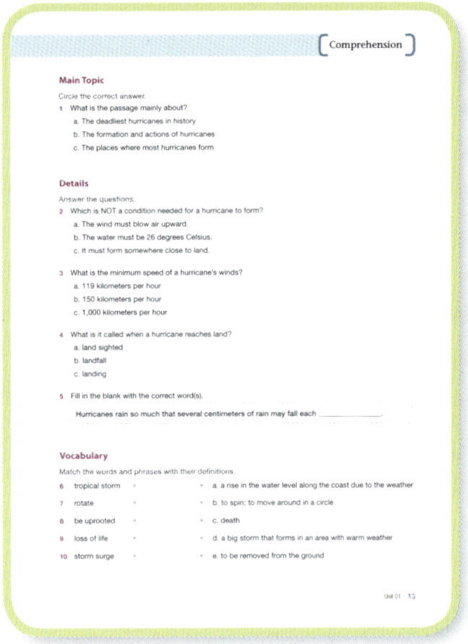

Comprehension

Main Topic

Circle the correct answer.

1 What is the passage mainly about?
a. The deadliest hurricanes in history
b. The formation and actions of hurricanes
c. The places where most hurricanes form

Details

Answer the questions.

2 Which is NOT a condition needed for a hurricane to form?
a. The wind must blow air upward.
b. The water must be 26 degrees Celsius.
c. It must form somewhere close to land.

3 What is the minimum speed of a hurricane's winds?
a. 119 kilometers per hour
b. 150 kilometers per hour
c. 1,000 kilometers per hour

4 What is it called when a hurricane reaches land?
a. land sighted
b. landfall
c. landing

5 Fill in the blank with the correct word(s).
Hurricanes rain so much that several centimeters of rain may fall each ________.

Vocabulary

Match the words and phrases with their definitions.

6 tropical storm • • a. a rise in the water level along the coast due to the weather
7 rotate • • b. to spin; to move around in a circle
8 be uprooted • • c. death
9 loss of life • • d. a big storm that forms in an area with warm weather
10 storm surge • • e. to be removed from the ground

Unit 01 · 13

Comprehension

This page contains several questions about the main passage. There is a question about the main topic or main idea of the passage. There are also four questions that ask about the details in the passage. Finally, there are five vocabulary questions for learners to test their knowledge of the words in the passage.

Reading Skills Practice

This section provides further practice for learners. First, there is a reading skills section in each unit. Various reading skills, such as sequencing, chronological order, cause and effect, and problem and solution, are covered in each unit. There is a description of the reading skill as well as questions for learners to test their understanding of the reading skill.

In addition, there is a short passage that is around 120-150 words long. Each passage provides information about a topic related to the main passage. There are comprehension questions and reading skill questions for each short passage as well.

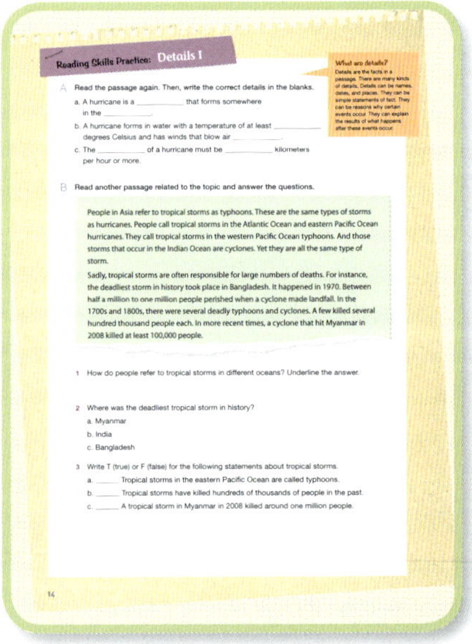

Reading Skills Practice: Details I

What are details?
Details are the facts in a passage. There are many kinds of details. Details can be names, dates, and places. They can be simple statements of fact. They can be reasons why certain events occur. They can explain the results of what happens after these events occur.

A Read the passage again. Then, write the correct details in the blanks.
a. A hurricane is a ________ that forms somewhere in the ________.
b. A hurricane forms in water with a temperature of at least ________ degrees Celsius and has winds that blow air ________.
c. The ________ of a hurricane must be ________ kilometers per hour or more.

B Read another passage related to the topic and answer the questions.

People in Asia refer to tropical storms as typhoons. These are the same types of storms as hurricanes. People call tropical storms in the Atlantic Ocean and eastern Pacific Ocean hurricanes. They call tropical storms in the western Pacific Ocean typhoons. And those storms that occur in the Indian Ocean are cyclones. Yet they are all the same type of storm.
Sadly, tropical storms are often responsible for large numbers of deaths. For instance, the deadliest storm in history took place in Bangladesh. It happened in 1970. Between half a million to one million people perished when a cyclone made landfall. In the 1700s and 1800s, there were several deadly typhoons and cyclones. A few killed several hundred thousand people each. In more recent times, a cyclone that hit Myanmar in 2008 killed at least 100,000 people.

1 How do people refer to tropical storms in different oceans? Underline the answer.

2 Where was the deadliest tropical storm in history?
a. Myanmar
b. India
c. Bangladesh

3 Write T (true) or F (false) for the following statements about tropical storms.
a. ______ Tropical storms in the eastern Pacific Ocean are called typhoons.
b. ______ Tropical storms have killed hundreds of thousands of people in the past.
c. ______ A tropical storm in Myanmar in 2008 killed around one million people.

14

C h a p t e r

1

Weather

UNIT 01

Hurricanes

Pre-Reading Questions

Answer the following questions.

1 What is happening in the picture?

2 Are there hurricanes in your country?

3 What happens during a hurricane?

4 Have you ever been in a violent storm? What was it like?

Vocabulary

Write the correct word or phrase from the box for each definition.

blow	evaporate	crash	landfall	massive	inland

1 ____________ to hit hard

2 ____________ to move like the wind

3 ____________ the act of arriving at or seeing land

4 ____________ away from the coast

5 ____________ to dry up; to change from a liquid to a gas

6 ____________ very large; huge

Hurricanes

Track 01

The sky becomes dark, and rain begins to fall heavily. The wind blows so hard that trees are uprooted. Waves three or four meters high begin crashing into the shore. Finally, a storm surge hits the beach and sends a huge wall of water inland. These are some of the effects of a hurricane.

Hurricanes are tropical storms that form in the Atlantic Ocean. There are several conditions necessary for them to form. First, they only form in water more than twenty-six degrees Celsius. They form when water that evaporates in these regions creates many clouds. Then, the wind must blow in a way that air moves both upward and begins to rotate. When that happens, a tropical storm has formed.

As the storm gains strength, it may become a hurricane. Hurricanes are measured by the speed of their winds. When the wind blows at least 119 kilometers per hour, the storm has become a hurricane. Some hurricanes have wind speeds more than 150 kilometers per hour. They may become massive in size as some are nearly 1,000 kilometers across. And they can last for days.

Many hurricanes never make landfall. Those that reach land can cause enormous amounts of damage. Some hurricanes drop ten or twenty centimeters of rain each hour. This amount of rain, combined with the storm surge, can cause flooding. This flooding often results in a great deal of damage and loss of life.

Summary

Read the summary. Write the correct word(s) from the box in each blank. You may need to change the forms of the words.

land	flooding	kilometer	tropical storm	damage

Sometimes storms cause heavy rain and wind and bring a lot of water onto ________________. These storms are hurricanes. Hurricanes are tropical storms that form in areas with warm water. They begin as ________________. As their wind speeds increase, they become hurricanes. Some hurricanes have winds that blow more than 150 ________________ per hour and are nearly 1,000 kilometers across. Hurricanes that make landfall can cause ________________. This can ________________ buildings and kill people.

Main Topic

Circle the correct answer.

1 What is the passage mainly about?

a. The deadliest hurricanes in history

b. The formation and actions of hurricanes

c. The places where most hurricanes form

Details

Answer the questions.

2 Which is NOT a condition needed for a hurricane to form?

a. The wind must blow air upward.

b. The water must be 26 degrees Celsius.

c. It must form somewhere close to land.

3 What is the minimum speed of a hurricane's winds?

a. 119 kilometers per hour

b. 150 kilometers per hour

c. 1,000 kilometers per hour

4 What is it called when a hurricane reaches land?

a. land sighted

b. landfall

c. landing

5 Fill in the blank with the correct word(s).

Hurricanes rain so much that several centimeters of rain may fall each ______________.

Vocabulary

Match the words and phrases with their definitions.

6	tropical storm	a. a rise in the water level along the coast due to the weather
7	rotate	b. to spin; to move around in a circle
8	be uprooted	c. death
9	loss of life	d. a big storm that forms in an area with warm weather
10	storm surge	e. to be removed from the ground

Reading Skills Practice: Details I

What are details?
Details are the facts in a passage. There are many kinds of details. Details can be names, dates, and places. They can be simple statements of fact. They can be reasons why certain events occur. They can explain the results of what happens after these events occur.

A **Read the passage again. Then, write the correct details in the blanks.**

a. A hurricane is a ____________ that forms somewhere in the ____________.

b. A hurricane forms in water with a temperature of at least ____________ degrees Celsius and has winds that blow air ____________.

c. The ____________ of a hurricane must be ____________ kilometers per hour or more.

B **Read another passage related to the topic and answer the questions.**

People in Asia refer to tropical storms as typhoons. These are the same types of storms as hurricanes. People call tropical storms in the Atlantic Ocean and eastern Pacific Ocean hurricanes. They call tropical storms in the western Pacific Ocean typhoons. And those storms that occur in the Indian Ocean are cyclones. Yet they are all the same type of storm.

Sadly, tropical storms are often responsible for large numbers of deaths. For instance, the deadliest storm in history took place in Bangladesh. It happened in 1970. Between half a million to one million people perished when a cyclone made landfall. In the 1700s and 1800s, there were several deadly typhoons and cyclones. A few killed several hundred thousand people each. In more recent times, a cyclone that hit Myanmar in 2008 killed at least 100,000 people.

1 How do people refer to tropical storms in different oceans? Underline the answer.

2 Where was the deadliest tropical storm in history?

a. Myanmar

b. India

c. Bangladesh

3 Write T (true) or F (false) for the following statements about tropical storms.

a. ______ Tropical storms in the eastern Pacific Ocean are called typhoons.

b. ______ Tropical storms have killed hundreds of thousands of people in the past.

c. ______ A tropical storm in Myanmar in 2008 killed around one million people.

UNIT 02 Tornadoes

Pre-Reading Questions

Answer the following questions.

1 What is a tornado?

2 How much damage can a tornado do?

3 Does your country get tornadoes?

4 What do you think it would be like to be near a tornado?

Vocabulary

Write the correct word or phrase from the box for each definition.

twister	regrettably	path	extend	destructive	fairly

1 ____________ to be wide; to stretch from one area to another

2 ____________ sadly; unfortunately

3 ____________ causing a great deal of damage

4 ____________ a tornado

5 ____________ a course; a way; a road

6 ____________ quite; rather

Tornadoes

Track **02**

In The Wizard of OZ, Dorothy and her dog Toto hide in a farmhouse to avoid a tornado. But the twister picks up the entire house and then gently lowers it to the ground in a distant land. Regrettably, tornadoes are not like that. They are powerful enough to move an entire house. But there is nothing gentle about them. Instead, they are among the most violent and destructive forces in nature.

Most tornadoes form during thunderstorms. The conditions for their formation are ideal then. Basically, warm air from one region and cold air from another area encounter each other. Then, the air begins to spin rapidly. A tornado can form from this spinning air. Tornadoes spin at very fast rates. Some of the most powerful ones have winds that move more than 500 kilometers per hour. Most tornadoes are fairly thin columns of air. Yet some can extend for two or three kilometers. These tornadoes utterly destroy anything in their paths.

One country that has a lot of tornadoes is the United States. A region of the country in the Midwest and Southeast gets many tornadoes. In fact, so many tornadoes happen there that it is called Tornado Alley. The states of Kansas and Oklahoma have the most tornadoes. Every spring, residents of the states in Tornado Alley always watch the sky when there are storm clouds in it.

Summary

Read the summary. Write the correct word(s) from the box in each blank. You may need to change the forms of the words.

blow	region	extend	rapidly	violent

Tornadoes are extremely ________________ and destructive forces of nature. They usually happen during thunderstorms. When warm air and hot air meet, the air might spin ________________. This can form a tornado. Some tornadoes have winds that ________________ more than 500 kilometers per hour. Most tornadoes are thin, but some may ________________ for two or three kilometers. Tornado Alley is a place in the United States that gets many tornadoes. People in that ________________ always watch out for tornadoes.

Main Topic

Circle the correct answer.

1 What is the main topic of the passage?

a. Tornadoes and how they form

b. The tornado in *The Wizard of OZ*

c. Why some tornadoes kill people

Details

Answer the questions.

2 When do tornadoes usually form?

a. During hurricanes

b. During snowstorms

c. During thunderstorms

3 Which of the following statements about tornadoes is true?

a. Their winds always blow more than 500 kilometers per hour.

b. The majority of them are thin columns of air.

c. They can pick up a house but not destroy it.

4 Which state is NOT in Tornado Alley?

a. California

b. Oklahoma

c. Kansas

5 Fill in the blank with the correct word(s).

Tornado Alley is a region in the ________________ that gets many tornadoes.

Vocabulary

Match the words and phrases with their definitions.

6	thunderstorm	a. totally; completely
7	utterly	b. a dark cloud that indicates it will rain soon
8	resident	c. a person who lives in a certain place
9	storm cloud	d. air that moves around in a circle
10	spinning air	e. a rainstorm with thunder and lightning

Reading Skills Practice: Details II

A Read the passage again. Then, write the correct details in the blanks.

a. Tornadoes can form when ____________ air in one place and ____________ air in another place meet.

b. Tornadoes ____________ very fast and can have ____________ that blow more than 500 kilometers per hour.

c. ____________ is in the American Midwest and Southeast and gets many tornadoes in the ____________.

What are details?
Details are the facts in a passage. There are many kinds of details. Details provide more information about the events in the passage. They can answer questions that begin with wh-question words such as *who*, *what*, *when*, *where*, *how*, and *why*.

B Read another passage related to the topic and answer the questions.

Dear Diary,

Last night was the most frightening moment of my life. Everyone in my family was watching TV in the living room. Suddenly, the power went out. A moment later, we heard sirens going off in the distance. Then, we heard a sound that was like the loudest freight train I had ever heard. My parents both yelled, "Tornado!" My brother and I didn't know what to do. My parents made us go down to the basement and hide underneath the big table there. All four of us remained there until we couldn't hear the tornado anymore. Then, we went upstairs. Our house was a mess. All of the windows were broken, and a tree had crashed through the roof. We went outside and saw it was even worse. Two of our neighbors' homes were totally destroyed. I couldn't believe my eyes.

1 What did the family do during the tornado? Underline the answer.

2 What did the tornado sound like?

a. A train

b. A siren

c. A TV

3 Write T (true) or F (false) for the following statements about the tornado.

a. ______ It broke the windows in the house.

b. ______ It knocked down several trees outside.

c. ______ It destroyed two houses in the area.

UNIT 03

The Water Cycle

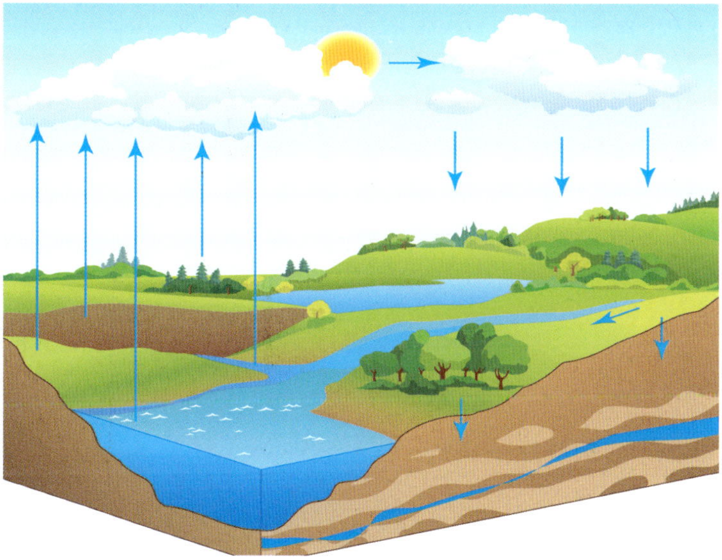

Pre-Reading Questions

Answer the following questions.

1 What is the water cycle?

2 Why is the water cycle important?

3 How much water is there on the planet?

4 Why do you think water is necessary for life? How do plants and animals use it?

Vocabulary

Write the correct word or phrase from the box for each definition.

soak	transform	condense	constant	unite	release

1 ____________ steady; regular

2 ____________ to change from a gas to a liquid

3 ____________ to let go

4 ____________ to absorb; to pass through or into

5 ____________ to come together; to join

6 ____________ to change; to alter

The Water Cycle

Track 03

The amount of water on the Earth is constant. But the water often changes its form. It does this in a process called the water cycle. There are four stages in the water cycle. They are evaporation, condensation, precipitation, and collection.

Evaporation is the process through which liquid water turns into water vapor. During the day, heat from the sun causes water in oceans, seas, rivers, and lakes to turn into steam. This steam is water vapor. The water vapor then rises into the air.

The next stage is condensation. The atmosphere has different temperatures. Closer to the ground, it is often warmer. As water vapor rises, it encounters colder air. This change in the temperature makes it transform back into liquid water. When this happens, the water condenses.

After that, numerous tiny droplets of water unite to form clouds. When a cloud becomes too heavy, it releases some of its water, which falls to the ground. It usually falls as rain. But it may also be snow, ice, hail, or sleet. This is known as precipitation.

The final stage is collection. Water, snow, or other precipitation may land in bodies of water. Then, it may once again evaporate. Or it may land on the ground. It may be drunk by animals, be used by plants, or soak into the groundwater beneath the surface. In this way, the water cycle continually reuses all of the water on the planet.

Summary

Read the summary. Write the correct word(s) from the box in each blank. You may need to change the forms of the words.

collection	rain	ocean	evaporate	cloud

The water cycle has four stages. The first is evaporation. This happens when water in ____________, seas, rivers, and lakes becomes water vapor and rises into the air. Next is condensation. The water vapor turns into water droplets, which unite to form ____________. The third stage is precipitation. This happens when ____________, snow, and other forms of water fall to the ground. The fourth stage is ____________. The water returns to the surface, where it can ____________ again.

Main Topic

Circle the correct answer.

1 What is the passage mainly about?

a. The different stages that water goes through

b. Why water evaporates and condenses

c. The amount of water on the Earth's surface

Details

Answer the questions.

2 What happens when water evaporates?

a. It changes from a solid to a liquid.

b. It changes from a liquid to a gas.

c. It changes from a gas to a solid.

3 What are rain, snow, and ice forms of?

a. Condensation

b. Precipitation

c. Evaporation

4 Which of the following does NOT happen to water after it falls to the ground?

a. It soaks into the ground.

b. It is consumed by animals.

c. It transforms into snow.

5 Fill in the blank with the correct word(s).

There are ________________ stages in the Earth's water cycle.

Vocabulary

Match the words and phrases with their definitions.

6	process	a. a very small drop
7	droplet	b. evaporated water that is in the air
8	groundwater	c. water beneath the Earth's surface
9	water vapor	d. small pieces of ice that fall as precipitation
10	hail	e. a method; a course; a development

Reading Skills Practice: Connecting Words I

What are connecting words?
Use connecting words to combine two or more words, sentences, or phrases. Connecting words let you put similar facts or opinions together. They also let you make comparisons and contrasts. Sometimes connecting words are at the beginning of a sentence. Some common connecting words are *in addition*, *in fact*, *also*, *when*, and *however*.

A **Read the passage again. Then, use the connecting words in the box to complete the sentences.**

When	But	In addition

a. There is a constant amount of water on the Earth. ____________ this water often changes forms.

b. ____________ water vapor encounters cold air, it transforms back into liquid form.

c. Water that falls as precipitation may land in bodies of water. ____________, it may soak into the ground.

B **Read another passage related to the topic and answer the questions.**

On most days, people can look at the sky and see clouds in it. Clouds are collections of tiny drops of water and crystals of ice. There are many different types of clouds. People can predict the type of weather that will occur simply by looking at them. For instance, clouds that are very high in the atmosphere are cirrus clouds. These white clouds are often indicators of pleasant weather. Yet they are also signs that there may be rain by the next day. Alto clouds, on the other hand, are clouds at medium altitudes. These clouds may cover the entire sky. In addition, they often indicate either thunderstorms or the continual falling of rain and snow. The lowest clouds in the sky are stratus clouds. They may sometimes indicate light rain. However, no precipitation usually falls from them.

1 Find the connecting words in the passage and circle them.

2 What are the lowest clouds?

a. Alto clouds

b. Stratus clouds

c. Cirrus clouds

3 Choose the correct connecting words for the sentences.

a. There are many kinds of clouds. (But / And) people can predict the weather by looking at the clouds.

b. Cirrus clouds often indicate that the weather is pleasant. (Or / Yet) they also indicate that it will rain soon.

c. Alto clouds are clouds at medium heights. (In addition / Therefore) they are signs it will rain or snow.

UNIT

04 Snow

Pre-Reading Questions

Answer the following questions.

1 What is the scene in each picture?

2 How often does it snow in your country?

3 What are some problems that snow can cause?

4 How do you like snow?

Vocabulary

Write the correct word or phrase from the box for each definition.

breathtaking	peak	light	impassable	snowstorm	frozen

1 ____________ a period when very much snow falls

2 ____________ not heavy; very little

3 ____________ beautiful; stunning

4 ____________ having turned solid due to the cold

5 ____________ the top of a mountain

6 ____________ unable to be crossed

Snow

Track **04**

Mother Nature can be both beautiful and deadly at the same time. This is definitely true when it comes to snow. A forest with trees covered with snow may be a breathtaking sight. But snow can also cause the deaths of many people.

Snow is a form of frozen precipitation. High in the atmosphere, when the temperature falls below zero degrees Celsius, the water in clouds turns into ice crystals. When a cloud becomes too heavy, it releases these crystals, so they fall to the ground. If the temperature from the cloud to the ground never rises above zero degrees, then the crystals will fall to the ground as snow.

Snow is common in places where the temperature is usually cold in winter. But it may also fall in more unusual areas. For example, it sometimes snows in hot deserts. And some of the mountains in Hawaii, a tropical paradise, are so high that snow falls at their peaks.

When the amount of snowfall is light, there are few problems. But some regions may get hit by snowstorms. In those instances, several centimeters of snow can fall in only a few hours. One problem with heavy snow is that snowdrifts several meters high may form. Heavy snowfall may make roads impassable. It may also knock down power lines. Homes and buildings may be damaged by too much snow. Sometimes people even die because of the snow.

Summary

Read the summary. Write the correct word(s) from the box in each blank. You may need to change the forms of the words.

ground	deadly	temperature	heavy	snowfall

Snow can be both beautiful and ______________. Snow can fall when the ______________ falls below zero degrees Celsius. Water in clouds turns into ice crystals, and these then fall to the ______________ as snow. Snow often falls in places with cold winters. Yet it can also fall in hot deserts and even in Hawaii at times. When ______________ is light, there are few problems. But ______________ snowfall can result in many problems, including the deaths of people.

Main Topic

Circle the correct answer.

1 What is the main topic of the passage?

a. The most unusual places that snow falls

b. How most people feel about snow

c. Why snow falls and the harm it can do

Details

Answer the questions.

2 What happens when the temperature in a cloud falls below zero degrees Celsius?

a. The cloud releases its water as rain.

b. The water in the cloud becomes ice crystals.

c. A large snowstorm begins.

3 Which is NOT mentioned as an unusual place where snow may fall?

a. Hawaii

b. Hot deserts

c. The beach

4 How high can some snowdrifts be?

a. Several centimeters

b. Several meters

c. Several kilometers

5 Fill in the blank with the correct word(s)

Snow can be a sight of ______________ beauty, but it can also be a deadly killer.

Vocabulary

Match the words and phrases with their definitions.

6	when it comes to	a. a line that carries electricity
7	snowdrift	b. an image of nature as a woman; nature
8	Mother Nature	c. concerning
9	power line	d. a beautiful area that has hot weather all year long
10	tropical paradise	e. a place where snow has piled up very high

Reading Skills Practice: Connecting Words II

What are connecting words?
Use connecting words to combine two or more words, sentences, or phrases. Connecting words let you put similar facts or opinions together. They also let you make comparisons and contrasts. Many times, connecting words are in the middle of a sentence. Some common connecting words are *and*, *but*, *so*, *or*, *when*, and *because*.

A Read the passage again. Then, use the correct connecting words in the box to complete the sentences.

and	but	when

a. Snow may be a breathtaking sight, ____________ it can also cause many people to die.

b. ____________ the temperature falls below zero degrees Celsius, snow may fall.

c. It sometimes snows both in hot deserts ____________ in tropical paradises such as Hawaii.

B Read another passage related to the topic and answer the questions.

Dear Gina,

I am having a great time in Switzerland. It is a beautiful country with lots of mountains. We have gone skiing a few times and mountain climbing once. That was a frightening experience because a blizzard happened then. Here is what happened: We were climbing a mountain when it started to snow. Our guide said it was not a problem, but he was wrong. Suddenly, the snow began falling heavily. We could not see a single thing. It was totally white. We were caught in a blizzard. Our guide yelled to us and told us not to move. I was so scared during the blizzard. Fortunately, it only lasted for around twenty minutes. When the blizzard ended, there was a lot of snow on the ground. I was really happy to get back to the hotel that day.

Your friend,
Mark

1 Find the connecting words in the passage and circle them.

2 What was Mark doing when the blizzard started?

a. He was climbing a mountain.

b. He was relaxing at a hotel.

c. He was skiing down a mountain.

3 Choose the correct connecting words for the sentences.

a. Mark went skiing several times (or / and) mountain climbing once.

b. The snow was falling heavily, (so / but) they could not see a single thing.

c. There was a lot of snow on the ground (because / when) the blizzard ended.

Chapter

2

Literature

UNIT

05 The Jungle Book

Pre-Reading Questions

Answer the following questions.

1 What can you see in the picture?

2 What kinds of animals live in the jungle?

3 Do you think it is possible for humans to live with animals?

4 What would it be like to grow up in the jungle?

Vocabulary

Write the correct word or phrase from the box for each definition.

publish	tale	obey	colony	influence	immediate

1 ____________ instant

2 ____________ to have an effect on

3 ____________ a story

4 ____________ to print, as in a book or a magazine

5 ____________ a land that belongs to or is ruled by another country

6 ____________ to follow; to listen to

The Jungle Book

Track 05

One of the best of all British writers was Rudyard Kipling. He lived from 1865 to 1936. Kipling led a unique life in that he did not always reside in Britain. Instead, he was born in India, which was a British colony at the time. He spent many years in India, and his time abroad greatly influenced his writing. It particularly influenced his work *The Jungle Book*. Many consider it among the greatest of Kipling's books.

Kipling published *The Jungle Book* in 1894. It is not a single tale. Instead, it is a collection of stories. Most of them are centered upon Mowgli. He is a young boy who is abandoned in a jungle of India. The boy is found and raised by wolves. During his time in the jungle, Mowgli has a number of adventures. **A** He is often helped by the bear Baloo and the black panther Bagheera. **B** Mowgli's greatest enemy is Shere Khan, a tiger that often tries to kill him. **C**

In *The Jungle Book*, the animals are able to communicate with Mowgli. The animals also follow the Law of the Jungle. It is a set of morals that most jungle animals, even Shere Khan, obey. Only the monkeys, who live above the jungle, do not follow it. *The Jungle Book* was an immediate success. In fact, it proved to be so popular that Kipling published *The Second Jungle Book* the next year.

Summary

Read the summary. Write the correct word(s) from the box in each blank. You may need to change the forms of the words.

raised	writer	success	enemy	collection

Rudyard Kipling was a British ________________ who lived in India for many years. He wrote *The Jungle Book* in 1894. It was a ________________ of tales mostly about Mowgli, a boy who grew up in the jungle. Mowgli is ________________ by wolves and communicates with many animals. His ________________ is the tiger Shere Khan. Most of the animals follow the Law of the Jungle. *The Jungle Book* was a ________________, so Kipling wrote a second book the next year.

Main Topic

Circle the correct answer.

1 What is the passage mainly about?

a. A book by Rudyard Kipling

b. The life of Rudyard Kipling

c. Rudyard Kipling and his works

Details

Answer the questions.

2 Where was Rudyard Kipling born?

a. In India

b. In Britain

c. In the United States

3 Which statement is true about Mowgli?

a. He is raised in the jungle by Shere Khan.

b. He gets help from a bear and a panther.

c. He hunts wolves that live in the jungle.

4 Which animals do NOT follow the Law of the Jungle?

a. The tigers

b. The bears

c. The monkeys

5 Fill in the blank with the correct word(s).

Mowgli is raised by ________________ and is able to communicate with the animals in the jungle.

Vocabulary

Match the words and phrases with their definitions.

6	reside	•	• a. to be about; to focus on
7	abandoned	•	• b. left alone
8	morals	•	• c. to live in a certain place; to dwell
9	be centered upon	•	• d. an opponent
10	enemy	•	• e. principles; a system of beliefs that describes what is right and what is wrong

Reading Skills Practice: Insert Text I

A Read the passage again. Then, decide where the sentence below best fits in the passage by choosing [A], [B], or [C].

Fortunately, Mowgli is always able to defeat his opponent.

a. [A]

b. [B]

c. [C]

> **What is insert text?**
> Use insert text to add a new sentence or sentences to a passage. Sometimes you want to make a passage longer. You must put the new sentence in the correct place. Read the passage carefully. Then, decide the best place for the new sentence.

B Read another passage related to the topic and answer the questions.

Another popular story from *The Jungle Book* is "Rikki-Tikki-Tavi." So many people enjoy it that it has been released as a book by itself and has been made into a movie. Rikki-Tikki-Tavi is the name of a mongoose. His name comes from the sounds that he makes. Rikki-Tikki-Tavi lives with a British couple and their son in India. There are a couple of cobras that live near the house. Their names are Nag and Nagaina. One night, Nag enters the house to try to kill the people, but Rikki-Tikki-Tavi kills him instead. Then, Rikki-Tikki-Tavi tries to destroy all of Nagaina's eggs. [A] He winds up having a fight with her in her underground lair. [B] He kills Nagaina and destroys all of her eggs. [C] Then, he determines to protect the area from any other cobras.

1 Where does the sentence below best fit in the passage?

He wants to do that to prevent even more cobras from living near the house.

a. [A]

b. [B]

c. [C]

2 What is Rikki-Tikki-Tavi?

a. A cobra

b. A panther

c. A mongoose

3 Where do Rikki-Tikki-Tavi and Nagaina fight?

a. In the garden

b. Underground

c. In the house

UNIT 06

Moby-Dick

Pre-Reading Questions

Answer the following questions.

1 What are the men in the picture doing?

2 What is the whale doing?

3 What is whaling? What is your opinion of whaling?

4 How would you like to go to sea for one or two years?

Vocabulary

Write the correct word or phrase from the box for each definition.

novel	revenge	battle	journey	recognize	announce

1 ____________ a book of fiction

2 ____________ to realize something; to see that something is true

3 ____________ a very long trip

4 ____________ to state out loud

5 ____________ payback; the act of getting back at someone for an act that person did

6 ____________ a fight

Moby-Dick

Track **06**

Many people have tried to write the great American novel. Herman Melville actually did it. Melville lived during the 1800s. It was an age of travel, and Melville spent several years exploring the world. He sailed on many ships in the Pacific Ocean. During his journeys, he had a number of adventures. He wrote about them in his early novels *Typee* and *Omoo*. These novels sold well, but they were not his greatest works. The novel that has made Melville recognized as one of the greatest of all American writers was *Moby-Dick*.

Moby-Dick is a novel about a hunt for a great white whale. It is narrated by Ishmael, one of the crew members of the *Pequod*, a whaling ship. The first line of the story—"Call me Ishmael"—is one of the most well-known opening lines in all literature. From the first line to the rest of the story, Melville tells an incredible tale about one man's quest for revenge.

Captain Ahab is the captain of the *Pequod*. He takes his crew to the Indian Ocean and announces that they are going to hunt for a white whale named Moby-Dick. It was Moby-Dick that caused Captain Ahab to lose his leg. [A] The crew searches for a long time, and they finally find the great white whale. [B] During a battle, Moby-Dick attacks the *Pequod* and sinks it. [C] Everyone on board, except for Ishmael, dies when the ship sinks.

Summary

Read the summary. Write the correct word(s) from the box in each blank. You may need to change the forms of the words.

travel	whale	sink	novel	great

Herman Melville ________________ throughout the Pacific Ocean by ship. He wrote the novels *Typee* and *Omoo* about his adventures there. Then, he wrote *Moby-Dick*. It was the ________________ American novel. *Moby-Dick* is the story of Captain Ahab's hunt for a great white ________________. The ________________ is about a man's quest for revenge. In the story, Moby-Dick ________________ the *Pequod* and kills everyone on the ship except for Ishmael, the narrator of the story.

Main Topic

Circle the correct answer.

1 What is the main topic of the passage?

a. Herman Melville and *Moby-Dick*

b. The life of Herman Melville

c. The importance of the book *Moby-Dick*

Details

Answer the questions.

2 Which of the following is NOT a novel by Herman Melville?

a. *Typee*

b. *Pequod*

c. *Omoo*

3 Who is Ishmael?

a. He is the narrator of the story.

b. He is the captain of the ship.

c. He is the person who finds Moby-Dick.

4 What happens at the end of the story?

a. Moby-Dick escapes, and Captain Ahab survives.

b. Captain Ahab finds and kills Moby-Dick.

c. Moby-Dick sinks the ship and kills most of the crew.

5 Fill in the blank with the correct word(s).

Herman Melville succeeded at writing the great American ______________ when he published *Moby-Dick*.

Vocabulary

Match the words and phrases with their definitions.

6	crew member	a. a journey in which a person searches for something
7	quest	b. a ship whose crew hunts and kills whales
8	tale	c. a story
9	be narrated by	d. a person who works on a ship
10	whaling ship	e. to be told by

Reading Skills Practice: Insert Text II

A Read the passage again. Then, decide where the sentence below best fits in the passage by choosing [A], [B], or [C].

However, their hunt for the great white whale is not successful.

a. [A]
b. [B]
c. [C]

What is insert text?
Use insert text to add a new sentence or sentences to a passage. Sometimes you want to make a passage longer. You must put the new sentence in the correct place. Many times, the new sentence has important connecting words such as *for example*, *then*, *therefore*, *instead*, and *however*. Use these words to help decide the best place for the new sentence.

B Read another passage related to the topic and answer the questions.

July 1, 1821, Nantucket, MA – News of the whaling ship *Essex* has just reached Nantucket, and the story is a sad one. The *Essex* set sail from Nantucket in 1819. Its destination was the rich whaling grounds of the South Pacific Ocean. It had a crew of twenty-one when it set sail. While hunting whales, the *Essex* itself was actually hunted. Apparently, a very large sperm whale—estimated to be more than twenty-five meters long—rammed the *Essex* twice. The whale, which was a large as the ship itself, caused the *Essex* to sink. There has never been a recorded instance of a whale attacking and sinking a ship like that. [A] Only eight of the crew survived the incident. [B] The others either perished when the ship sank or died elsewhere in the Pacific Ocean. [C]

1 Where does the sentence below best fit in the passage?

Therefore, this appears to be a unique event.

a. [A]
b. [B]
c. [C]

2 What caused the *Essex* to sink?

a. A submarine
b. A bomb
c. A whale

3 How many crew members on the *Essex* survived?

a. Eight
b. Thirteen
c. Twenty-one

UNIT 07 William Shakespeare

Pre-Reading Questions

Answer the following questions.

1 What can you see in each picture?

2 Who was William Shakespeare?

3 What else do you know about William Shakespeare?

4 How do you like watching plays?

Vocabulary

Write the correct word or phrase from the box for each definition.

poet	audience	perform	rhyme	genre	tragedy

1 ____________ to act

2 ____________ a drama; an unfortunate event

3 ____________ a kind; a type

4 ____________ a person who writes poems

5 ____________ to sound alike

6 ____________ the people who are watching a performance or sporting event

William Shakespeare

Track 07

There have been many excellent British writers. They include John Milton, Charles Dickens, and William Wordsworth. But the greatest of all of them was William Shakespeare. He was born in 1564 and died in 1616. Very little is known about his life. He was from the town of Stratford but later moved to London. He was not only a writer but was also an actor. Shakespeare often even performed roles in the plays he wrote.

Shakespeare is mostly famous for his plays. During his life, he composed thirty-seven plays. Shakespeare's plays can be divided into three separate genres. They are history, comedy, and tragedy. Some of his most famous works are tragedies. These include *Romeo and Juliet*, *Macbeth*, and *Hamlet*. As for his comedies, *A Midsummer Night's Dream* is his greatest play. *Much Ado about Nothing* and *The Comedy of Errors* are two more comedies that audiences frequently enjoy.

While Shakespeare wrote plays, he was also an accomplished poet. He wrote a large number of poems. The most well-known poems he wrote were sonnets. He composed 154 sonnets during his lifetime. A sonnet is a poem that has fourteen lines. Each line of the sonnet contains a total of ten syllables. And the final words in the last two lines always rhyme. Most of Shakespeare's sonnets were about love. Sonnets 18, 29, and 138 are three of his best poems.

Summary

Read the summary. Write the correct word(s) from the box in each blank. You may need to change the forms of the words.

comedy   tragedy   line   greatest   poem

William Shakespeare was born in 1564 and died in 1616. He came from Stratford but moved to London. Shakespeare is considered the ________________ of all British writers. He wrote thirty-seven plays in three genres: history, ________________, and tragedy. *Romeo and Juliet* is one famous ________________ while *A Midsummer Night's Dream* is a well-known comedy. Shakespeare also wrote ________________. He wrote 154 sonnets, which are poems with fourteen ________________. Many of his sonnets are about love.

Main Topic

Circle the correct answer.

1 What is the main topic of the passage?

a. The important events in William Shakespeare's life

b. The people who influenced the work of William Shakespeare

c. The types of works that William Shakespeare wrote

Details

Answer the questions.

2 What type of play is *Macbeth*?

a. A comedy

b. A tragedy

c. A history

3 Which of the following is NOT true about sonnets?

a. Each line has ten syllables in it.

b. The last word in every line rhymes.

c. They are poems with fourteen lines.

4 What were Shakespeare's sonnets mostly about?

a. Love

b. Death

c. Marriage

5 Fill in the blank with the correct word(s).

William Shakespeare is considered the greatest of all British ________________.

Vocabulary

Match the words and phrases with their definitions.

6	accomplished	a. to be separated
7	sonnet	b. outstanding; excellent; talented
8	syllable	c. a character
9	be divided into	d. a short, complete sound in a language
10	role	e. a type of poem that has fourteen lines

Reading Skills Practice: Classification I

What is classification?
Use classification to put people, places, or things into groups. Many passages include information about two or more groups. These groups often have their own characteristics. Read the passage carefully. Then, put each characteristic into the correct group. Classification can help you understand more about people, places, or things.

A Read the passage again. Then, complete the classification charts.

Shakespeare's Plays

- Composed thirty-seven plays
- Wrote in 3 genres: a. ______________, comedy, and tragedy
- Tragedies include *Romeo and Juliet*, *Macbeth*, and b. ______________
- Greatest c. ______________ is *A Midsummer Night's Dream*

Shakespeare's Sonnets

- Wrote 154 sonnets
- Are poems with d. ______________ lines
- Each line has ten e. ______________
- Final words in last two lines f. ______________
- Wrote about love
- Sonnets 18, 29, and 138 are among best

B Read another passage related to the topic and answer the questions.

William Shakespeare lived during the Renaissance in England. During that time, many people began composing plays. Christopher Marlowe was one of these men. Like Shakespeare, Marlowe was born in the year 1564. However, he never achieved the great fame that Shakespeare did. One reason was that he died at the young age of twenty-nine. He was killed during a fight in a bar. Despite dying young, Marlowe wrote several plays that showed his great talent. Most of them were tragedies. For example, one of his best plays—and maybe the first one he wrote—was *Dido, Queen of Carthage*. He also composed the tragedy *Tamburlaine the Great*, which was about the emperor Timur. His most famous play was *Doctor Faustus*. In this drama, Faustus sells his soul to the Devil. In return, he receives both knowledge and power.

1 Underline the sentences that describe the tragedies of Christopher Marlowe.

2 Why did Christopher Marlowe fail to achieve the fame that William Shakespeare did?

a. Few people performed his plays.

b. He died at a young age.

c. He was not very talented.

3 Complete the classification chart about Christopher Marlowe's tragedies.

Christopher Marlowe's Tragedies

- Showed his great a. ______________
- Wrote *Dido, Queen of Carthage*
- Composed *Tamburlaine the Great* about the b. ______________ Timur
- Wrote *Doctor Faustus*
- Faustus sells his soul to the c. ______________ for knowledge and d. ______________

UNIT

08 Edgar Allan Poe

Pre-Reading Questions

Answer the following questions.

1 What can you see in the picture on the right?

2 Who was Edgar Allan Poe?

3 How do you like horror stories?

4 Do you know any famous horror stories?

Vocabulary

Write the correct word or phrase from the box for each definition.

essay	mysterious	frighten	alcoholism	investigator	struggle

1 ____________ to scare; to make afraid

2 ____________ an addiction to drinking alcohol

3 ____________ a piece of writing that attempts to convince the reader of something

4 ____________ to try hard

5 ____________ a detective; a person who tries to solve crimes

6 ____________ strange; unknown; unexplained

Edgar Allan Poe

Track 08

Some writers focus on a single genre while others write in two or more of them. Edgar Allan Poe was the second kind of writer. He was extremely versatile and produced many types of writing, including poems, short stories, and essays.

Most of Poe's works had dark themes and focused on death. This is especially true of his poems. *The Raven* is Poe's best-known poem. It is a poem about death and how a man struggles to accept the loss of his love. Many of Poe's other poems are also about death. Among them are *Lenore*, *Annabel Lee*, and *The City in the Sea*.

Poe wrote numerous short stories, too. One genre he frequently wrote in was horror. His short stories were often intended to frighten people. These works contained supernatural elements, which made them mysterious. *The Black Cat*, *The Masque of the Red Death*, and *The Fall of the House of Usher* are three of his best horror stories.

Not all of Poe's stories were scary though. He wrote detective stories as well. In fact, Poe invented that genre. His detective stories were about the investigator C. Auguste Dupin. *The Purloined Letter* and *The Murders in the Rue Morgue* were two of Poe's detective stories.

Sadly, Poe led a difficult life. His wife died at a young age, and he battled issues such as alcoholism and gambling. Poe himself died in 1849 at the age of forty.

Summary

Read the summary. Write the correct word(s) from the box in each blank. You may need to change the forms of the words.

horror	die	invent	theme	supernatural

Edgar Allan Poe wrote many different types of literature. His ________________ were often dark and about death. He wrote many poems like that. *The Raven* and *Annabel Lee* are two of his poems about death. Poe wrote short stories in the ________________ genre. His stories often have ________________ elements in them. Poe ________________ the detective story genre with his stories about C. Auguste Dupin. He led a difficult life and ________________ at the age of forty.

Main Topic

Circle the correct answer.

1 What is the passage mainly about?

a. The poetry of Edgar Allan Poe

b. Edgar Allan Poe's greatest works

c. The genres Edgar Allan Poe wrote in

Details

Answer the questions.

2 What is Edgar Allan Poe's best-known poem?

a. *Annabel Lee*

b. *Lenore*

c. *The Raven*

3 Which statement about Edgar Allan Poe's short stories is true?

a. His stories were often in the horror genre.

b. He only wrote detective stories.

c. He wrote nonfiction stories about people.

4 Which story by Edgar Allan Poe is NOT a detective story?

a. *The Fall of the House of Usher*

b. *The Murders in the Rue Morgue*

c. *The Purloined Letter*

5 Fill in the blank with the correct word(s).

> **Edgar Allan Poe was a versatile writer who created works of literature in a number of different ________________.**

Vocabulary

Match the words and phrases with their definitions.

6	be intended to	a. a topic that is gloomy or mysterious
7	supernatural element	b. flexible; able to change easily
8	horror	c. to be meant to
9	dark theme	d. terror; something that is very frightening
10	versatile	e. a strange or mysterious aspect

Reading Skills Practice: Classification II

What is classification?
Use classification to put information about a person, place, or thing into different categories. People, places, and things often have different features. Read the passage carefully. Then, put each feature into the correct classification. Classification can help you understand more about the person, place, or thing.

A Read the passage again. Then, complete the classification charts.

Edgar Allan Poe's Poems

- Had dark a. ______________
- Focused on b. ______________
- Best-known work is *The Raven*
- Also wrote c. ______________, *Annabel Lee*, and *The City in the Sea*

Edgar Allan Poe's Short Stories

- Frequently wrote horror stories
- Contained d. ______________ elements
- e. ______________ the detective story genre
- Wrote about the f. ______________ C. Auguste Dupin

B Read another passage related to the topic and answer the questions.

The Detective Stories of Edgar Allan Poe

a report by Nancy Davis

Edgar Allan Poe wrote all kinds of short stories. Some of his most influential short stories featured the detective C. Auguste Dupin. Dupin appeared in *The Purloined Letter*, *The Murders in the Rue Morgue*, and one other story. It was in these stories that Poe created the modern detective novel.

The Purloined Letter is a tale about a stolen letter. In this story, a letter that belongs to a lady is stolen by a minister in the government. Dupin manages to get the letter back in the story. In *The Murders in the Rue Morgue*, two women are killed in Paris. Dupin determines that it was no man, but an orangutan, that killed the women. In both stories, Dupin uses logic to solve the mysteries. I enjoyed how Dupin solved both cases.

1 Underline the sentences that describe *The Purloined Letter*. Circle the sentences that describe *The Murders in the Rue Morgue*.

2 How does Dupin solve the mysteries in the stories?

a. By calling the police

b. By using logic

c. By making guesses

3 Complete the classification charts.

The Purloined Letter

- About a a. ______________ letter
- The letter is stolen by a b. ______________
- Belongs to a c. ______________
- Dupin gets the letter back

The Murders in the Rue Morgue

- Two d. ______________ are killed in Paris
- Dupin learns who killed them
- Was not a e. ______________
- Was an f. ______________ that killed them

Chapter

3

Modern Technology

UNIT 09

Henry Ford and the Assembly Line

Pre-Reading Questions

Answer the following questions.

1 What is happening in the picture?

2 How does an assembly line work?

3 Who was Henry Ford? What did he do?

4 Who are some important businesspeople in your country's history?

Vocabulary

Write the correct word or phrase from the box for each definition.

forever	found	afford	nevertheless	manufacture	install

1 ____________ for all time

2 ____________ however; yet

3 ____________ to set up; to put in

4 ____________ to start a business, school, or other similar place

5 ____________ to have enough money to buy something

6 ____________ to make; to build

Henry Ford and the Assembly Line

Track 09

People often believe that Henry Ford invented the automobile. That is not true. Nevertheless, Henry Ford greatly influenced the automotive industry. He also had a great effect on the mass production of goods.

Henry Ford founded the Ford Motor Company and made his first car in 1903. It was called the Model A. For the next few years, Ford continued developing new cars. His goal was to manufacture a car that the majority of Americans could afford. In 1908, his company produced the first Model T. It cost $825. The company sold more than 10,000 Model T's the first year. Each year, the car became more and more popular.

The Model T became so popular that the Ford Motor Company could not produce enough of them. The demand was much greater than the supply. So Ford introduced a new assembly method to his factories. It was called the assembly line. First, he installed a moving belt. Then, the body of a car was put on it. Each worker along the assembly line had a single job to do. The belt slowly moved cars down the line. Then, each worker did his job. Thanks to the assembly line, the workers built cars much more quickly than before. Eventually, more than 15,000,000 Model T's were made. Other companies began using the assembly line to make their products, too. Thanks to Henry Ford, the history of mass production changed forever.

Summary

Read the summary. Write the correct word(s) from the box in each blank. You may need to change the forms of the words.

popular	found	assembly line	automobile	belt

Henry Ford did not invent the ________________, but he greatly influenced the automotive industry. Ford ________________ the Ford Motor Company. It started making cars in 1903. In 1908, it produced the first Model T. The Model T quickly became so ________________ that the company could not make enough of them. Ford then introduced the ________________. It was a moving ________________ that let workers manufacture cars more quickly than before. Overall, more than 15,000,000 Model T's were made.

Main Topic

Circle the correct answer.

1 What is the passage mainly about?

a. How Henry Ford affected the automotive industry

b. The early life and activities of Henry Ford

c. Why most factories use assembly lines today

Details

Answer the questions.

2 What was the first car that the Ford Motor Company made?

a. The Model T

b. The Model N

c. The Model A

3 Why did Henry Ford introduce the assembly line to his factories?

a. To increase production

b. To lower the supply

c. To reduce the number of workers

4 Which statement about the Model T is NOT true?

a. It took two days to make one Model T.

b. More than fifteen million Model T's were made.

c. It cost $825 when it came out in 1908.

5 Fill in the blank with the correct word(s).

Henry Ford changed the way that companies mass-produced goods by introducing the ______________.

Vocabulary

Match the words and phrases with their definitions.

6	demand	a. a way of making or building something
7	mass production	b. the desire to buy or have something
8	assembly method	c. the building of a large number of goods
9	majority	d. after some time; finally
10	eventually	e. more than fifty percent; most

Reading Skills Practice: Sequencing I

What is sequencing?
Use sequencing to put events in order. Start with the first event. Then, continue with the events in order until you have written everything. People often use sequencing words. Some sequencing words are *first*, *next*, *then*, *after that*, and *finally*.

A Read the passage again. Then, put the sentences in the correct order.

a. _______ The Model T became so popular that the company could not make enough.

b. _______ After that, workers could build cars much more quickly than before.

c. _______ Then, Henry Ford introduced a new assembly method to his factories.

B Read another passage related to the topic and answer the questions.

William Boeing was the owner of a lumber company. In 1909, he visited Seattle on business. There, he saw his first airplane. He became interested in them. So he purchased one for himself. Boeing flew his airplane so much that he broke it. It needed new parts, but he learned that the parts would not arrive for several months. Boeing became upset and claimed that he could build a better airplane much faster. Then, he founded his own airplane company in 1917. At first, Boeing made military aircraft since the United States was fighting World War I. After that, his company built commercial aircraft. It quickly became a leader in the aircraft industry. In 1954, the company made its first jet. Today, the Boeing Company is the largest aerospace company in the world and makes hundreds of planes every year.

1 Find the sequencing words in the passage and circle them.

2 What did William Boeing do in Seattle in 1909?

a. He purchased a lumber company.

b. He went for a ride in an airplane.

c. He saw an airplane for the first time.

3 Put the following sentences in the correct order.

a. _______ Then, his company began making military aircraft.

b. _______ Next, it made commercial aircraft after the war ended.

c. _______ First, Boeing founded an airplane company in 1917.

UNIT 10

Tim Berners-Lee and the World Wide Web

Pre-Reading Questions

Answer the following questions.

1 How was the World Wide Web (WWW) made?

2 When did you first go online? How was it?

3 What do you use the Internet for?

4 What are the good and bad points of the Internet?

Vocabulary

Write the correct word or phrase from the box for each definition.

complicated	laboratory	hypertext	war	suggest	link

1 ____________ an extended period of fighting between two or more countries

2 ____________ a room where a person conducts research

3 ____________ to connect; to join

4 ____________ complex; difficult

5 ____________ a way to store data on a computer that involves using links

6 ____________ to recommend; to advise

Tim Berners-Lee and the World Wide Web

Track **10**

In the 1960s, the United States and the Soviet Union were enemies. There was a constant threat that the two countries would fight a war with each other. The American government was worried about that. So the government wanted a way to communicate with people around the country in case there was a war. Researchers started to think of how to link computers to one another.

In 1969, ARPANET went online. It connected four computers at four universities in the United States. Then, in 1970, a few more university computers were added. Every year after that, more university computers were linked to each other. This was the earliest version of the Internet.

The first email was sent in 1972. During the 1970s, there were a few developments to the Internet. Then, in the 1980s, many people started to buy personal computers. Still, for the most part, only the government, universities, and large companies used the Internet. It was too complicated for most people to use.

This changed in 1989 thanks to Tim Berners-Lee. He was a researcher at CERN. It is a physics laboratory in Switzerland. First, he suggested building a system in which computers around the world were connected. This would let people share information. Then, he used hypertext to create the World Wide Web. After that, he created the world's first webpage. Today, because of Tim Berners-Lee, billions of people around the world have access to the World Wide Web.

Summary

Read the summary. Write the correct word(s) from the box in each blank. You may need to change the forms of the words.

create	communication	version	connect	webpage

In the 1960s, the United States government wanted a new ______________ system in case of war. Its researchers decided to ______________ computers to one another. ARPANET went online in 1969. It was the first ______________ of the Internet. In the 1970s and 1980s, the Internet continued to develop, but it was very complicated. Then, in 1989, Tim Berners-Lee ______________ the World Wide Web. He did that by using hypertext. He also created the world's first ______________.

Comprehension

Main Topic

Circle the correct answer.

1 What is the main topic of the passage?

a. The life of Tim Berners-Lee

b. The history of the Internet

c. What the World Wide Web is

Details

Answer the questions.

2 Where was the Internet created?

a. The Soviet Union

b. Switzerland

c. The United States

3 What was true about the Internet in the 1980s?

a. People could access it with their personal computers.

b. It was too complicated, so most people did not use it.

c. Only students at universities used the Internet.

4 Which of the following did Tim Berners-Lee NOT do?

a. He made the first webpage.

b. He invented the Internet.

c. He created the World Wide Web.

5 Fill in the blank with the correct word(s).

The Internet was created in the 1960s while the ______________ was made in 1989.

Vocabulary

Match the words and phrases with their definitions.

6	threat	a. to use; to be able to use
7	version	b. a computer meant to be used by an individual
8	personal computer	c. to give to others for free
9	share	d. a form
10	have access to	e. danger; a risk

Reading Skills Practice: Sequencing II

What is sequencing?
Use sequencing to put events in order. Start with the first event. Then, continue with the events in order until you have written everything. Sequencing words make reading a passage easier. Some sequencing words are *at first*, *later*, *after a while*, and *last*.

A Read the passage again. Then, put the sentences in the correct order.

a. _______ Then, Tim Berners-Lee invented the World Wide Web in 1989.

b. _______ First, ARPANET was created in 1969.

c. _______ After a while, many computers were connected to each other.

B Read another passage related to the topic and answer the questions.

Dear Diary,

I read an interesting article today. It was about Bill Gates. He is the one of the richest men in the world today. Here is how he became so rich. First, he became interested in computers when he was young. In fact, he started programming computers when he was only thirteen years old. Next, he went to Harvard University in 1973. At Harvard, he developed his own computer language. But he was not happy at Harvard. So, after a while, he quit going to school. Then, he focused on working at his company Microsoft. Gates started Microsoft with Paul Allen in 1975. After that, they began to develop software for personal computers. Their software became very popular in the 1980s and 1990s. So Bill Gates made a huge amount of money. He proved you can become rich through hard work.

1 Find the sequencing words in the passage and circle them.

2 What did Bill Gates and Paul Allen do?

a. They grew up together.

b. They started a company together.

c. They went to school together.

3 Put the following sentences in the correct order.

a. _______ Bill Gates quit going to Harvard.

b. _______ Bill Gates developed software for personal computers.

c. _______ Bill Gates started Microsoft in 1975.

UNIT 11

Satellites

Pre-Reading Questions

Answer the following questions.

1 Where is the satellite?

2 What can satellites do?

3 How do satellites get into outer space?

4 Do you think that satellites are useful to people?

Vocabulary

Write the correct word or phrase from the box for each definition.

manmade	device	mission	run	chart	predict

1 ____________ to operate

2 ____________ a job; a task

3 ____________ to diagram; to plot; to take notes on

4 ____________ artificial; anything that is not naturally made

5 ____________ to guess; to make a guess about the future

6 ____________ equipment; a tool

Satellites

Track 11

On October 4, 1957, the Space Age began. That day, the Soviet Union launched the artificial satellite *Sputnik*. It made each orbit of Earth in about ninety-eight minutes. It sent information back to the ground for about three weeks. And it stayed in orbit until January 1958. After *Sputnik*, space agencies all around the world began to launch satellites. Since 1957, thousands of satellites have been sent into space. At present, there are around 3,000 of them circling the planet.

A satellite is any object that orbits another. There are natural satellites. For instance, Earth is a satellite of the sun. And the moon is a satellite of Earth. There are also artificial satellites. These are manmade devices.

People use satellites for a large number of purposes. For instance, the modern telecommunications industry runs thanks to them. As a result, people can use mobile phones. They can watch cable TV. And they can connect to the Internet by using Wi-Fi. Satellites can help people predict the weather. Navigation systems in cars run thanks to them. The militaries of many countries use them to spy on their enemies. And many are used to do research. For instance, some observe the erupting of volcanoes. Others watch the melting and freezing of ocean ice. And some even chart the flowing of rivers and streams. Satellites are able to do a wide variety of missions.

Summary

Read the summary. Write the correct word(s) from the box in each blank. You may need to change the forms of the words.

artificial	research	orbit	weather	telecommunications

The Space Age began in 1957 when the Soviet Union launched the satellite *Sputnik*. Since then, thousands of ________________ satellites have been launched. They are manmade devices that ________________ other objects. Satellite can do many things. The ________________ and cable TV industries run thanks to them. Satellites can predict the ________________ and run navigation systems. Militaries use them to spy on their enemies. And they are valuable for doing all kinds of ________________, too.

Main Topic

Circle the correct answer.

1 What is the passage mainly about?

a. What satellites are and how they are used

b. When people began building artificial satellites

c. How satellites are launched into orbit

Details

Answer the questions.

2 What was *Sputnik*?

a. A natural satellite

b. A spy satellite

c. An artificial satellite

3 Which statement about satellites is correct?

a. There are more natural satellites than artificial satellites.

b. There are around 3,000 artificial satellites in orbit today.

c. The Soviet Union launched more satellites than any other country.

4 Which of the following do satellites NOT do?

a. Assist the telecommunications industry

b. Observe volcanoes that erupt

c. Help ice freeze and melt

5 Fill in the blank with the correct word(s).

Ever since the first ________________ was launched, people have used them to do many different tasks.

Vocabulary

Match the words and phrases with their definitions.

6	natural satellite	a. a cellular telephone
7	mobile phone	b. an organization concerned with studying and working in space
8	Wi-Fi	c. a natural object that orbits another
9	artificial satellite	d. a manmade object that orbits another
10	space agency	e. wireless fidelity; the ability to access the Internet without cables

Reading Skills Practice: Summarizing I

A **Read the passage again. Then, choose the correct summary sentence.**

a. Some satellites are used to do research, and others are used by countries' militaries.

b. There are thousands of satellites orbiting the Earth, and they have a variety of missions.

c. *Sputnik* was launched in October 1957, and that was the beginning of the Space Age.

What is summarizing?
Use summarizing to determine the main point of the passage. To summarize a passage, remove the minor details and unimportant information. Then, think about the most important ideas and details in the passage. Try to put them into one sentence. This is the summary sentence.

B **Read another passage related to the topic and answer the questions.**

In the early years of the Space Age, many satellites were sent into space. Astronauts were also sent into space. But they only remained in orbit for a few hours or days. People desired a more permanent presence in space. So they wanted to build space stations. A space station is a spacecraft that can stay in orbit for a long time. People live and work on space stations. In the 1970s, the Americans sent *Skylab* into orbit. It orbited the Earth from 1973 to 1979. The Soviets had several space stations. They included the *Almaz* stations, the *Salyut* stations, and *Mir*. Currently, there are two space stations in orbit. They are the *International Space Station* and the Chinese space station *Tiangong-1*. Astronauts live on these space stations for extended periods of time. And they conduct many valuable experiments on them.

1 Find the main details in the passage and underline them.

2 Which space station is orbiting the Earth today?

a. *Almaz*

b. *Tiangong-1*

c. *Skylab*

3 Choose the correct summary sentence.

a. *Skylab* was an American space station while *Mir* was a Soviet one.

b. Many countries worked together to send the *International Space Station* into space.

c. The countries of the world have sent many space stations into orbit.

UNIT 12

The Industrial Revolution

Pre-Reading Questions

Answer the following questions.

1 What can you see in each picture?

2 What was the Industrial Revolution?

3 How did the Industrial Revolution change society?

4 What do you think the most important invention during the Industrial Revolution was?

Vocabulary

Write the correct word or phrase from the box for each definition.

educated	textile	vital	undergo	factory	rural

1 ____________ to happen; to experience

2 ____________ learned; smart

3 ____________ related to the country

4 ____________ cloth; clothing

5 ____________ a place where products are manufactured

6 ____________ important

The Industrial Revolution

Track 12

For thousands of years, human society was based on farming. Most people lived in rural areas. They grew crops and raised animals. There were very few machines during that time. But this began to change in the 1700s. Suddenly, people started to invent a large number of machines. As a result, society changed. It became more industrial. Then, people left the countryside. They moved to large cities. This period was the Industrial Revolution.

The Industrial Revolution began in England. There were several reasons for this. First, England had large amounts of coal and iron. These were needed to industrialize. The English people were educated and liked making new machines. England also had many colonies. It imported great amounts of raw materials from them. So the factories had many raw materials to use.

There were many important inventions in the Industrial Revolution. The steam engine was among the most vital. It let people run machines without using wind, water, animal, or human power. The first steam engine was made in 1712. After that, people in England began to make factories. They used steam engines to run the machines in the factories.

A lot of industries were affected by the Industrial Revolution. Three were the textile, manufacturing, and farming industries. New methods of transportation were created, too. Overall, society underwent a great amount of change during this time. And it happened due to all the inventions made during this period.

Summary

Read the summary. Write the correct word from the box in each blank. You may need to change the forms of the words.

colony	manufacturing	farming	invention	England

Before the 1700s, human society was based on ________________. After that, the Industrial Revolution began. The Industrial Revolution started in ________________ for many reasons. Two were that the English people were educated and the country had ________________ that provided raw materials. The steam engine was the most important ________________. It was used in many factories. The textile, ________________, and farming industries were affected by the Industrial Revolution. It caused society to change a great deal.

Main Topic

Circle the correct answer.

1 What is the main topic of the passage?

a. The effects of the Industrial Revolution in England

b. The most important machines of the Industrial Revolution

c. The changes that happened during the Industrial Revolution

Details

Answer the questions.

2 What happened when the Industrial Revolution began?

a. Many people moved to cities.

b. Everyone worked in factories.

c. Farming became unpopular.

3 Which is NOT a reason the Industrial Revolution started in England?

a. The English people were well educated.

b. Raw materials in England were cheap.

c. England had a lot of iron and coal.

4 What was one of the most important inventions in the Industrial Revolution?

a. The steam engine

b. The airplane

c. The train

5 Fill in the blank with the correct word(s).

The Industrial Revolution helped change the world from one based on ____________ to one based on manufacturing.

Vocabulary

Match the words and phrases with their definitions.

6	countryside	a. to start to build factories and other industries
7	be based on	b. a natural material used to make other products
8	grow crops	c. a place in the country; a rural area
9	industrialize	d. to farm the land
10	raw material	e. to depend on

Reading Skills Practice: Summarizing II

A Read the passage again. Then, choose the correct summary sentence.

a. Many inventions were made in the Industrial Revolution, and they helped change a lot of different industries.

b. The Industrial Revolution started in England in the 1700s and then spread to other countries around the world.

c. Because of the steam engine, people were able to make large factories to manufacture goods in.

What is summarizing?
Use summarizing to determine the main point of the passage. To summarize a passage, remove the minor details and unimportant information. Then, think about the most important ideas and details in the passage. Be sure to use the key words and ideas from the passage when you make the summary sentence.

B Read another passage related to the topic and answer the questions.

August 21, 1750
Dear Mother,
All three of us have arrived in London a month ago. We have found jobs at a nearby factory. We work inside the factory making textiles all day long. We work long hours. We sometimes work up to sixteen hours a day. The factory is also not very clean, and it is dark inside, too. But we get paid, so we are happy. My brothers and I live in a small place near our factory. Lots of other workers from the factory live nearby. We are sorry that we did not stay on the farm with you and Father. But we felt that we had to get away from the countryside. Because of the new machines, fewer people are needed on farms these days. And factories in London are always hiring new workers.
Your son,
Ian

1 Find the key words and ideas in the passage and circle them.

2 What does Ian write about the factory he works in?

a. It is large.
b. It is clean.
c. It is dark.

3 Choose the correct summary sentence.

a. There are fewer jobs in the countryside, so people are moving to cities.
b. Ian and his brothers left the farm to find work at a factory in London.
c. People have to work very long hours in the factories in London.

Chapter

4

Economics

UNIT 13 The Silk Road

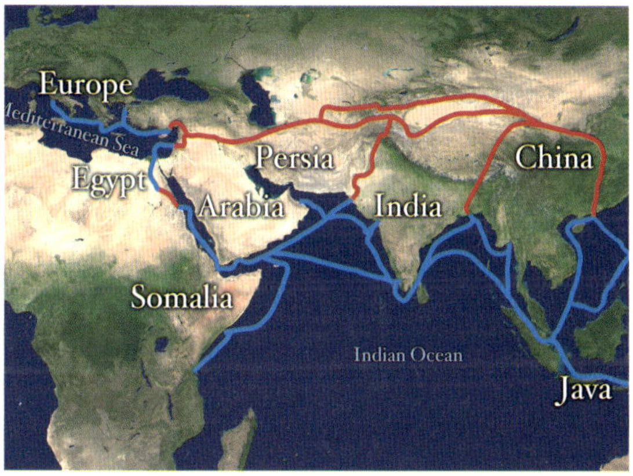

Pre-Reading Questions

Answer the following questions.

1 What are the people in the first picture doing?

2 Where was the Silk Road?

3 What do you think people traded on the Silk Road?

4 How do you think life on the Silk Road was?

Vocabulary

Write the correct word or phrase from the box for each definition.

destination	bandit	desired	typically	major	route

1 ____________ wanted

2 ____________ a road; a path

3 ____________ usually; normally

4 ____________ a thief; a robber

5 ____________ big; important

6 ____________ the place where one is going

The Silk Road

Track 13

People have always traded with each other. Typically, someone has an item that another person wants. So the second person offers to trade something else for that item. In the past, people usually traded with individuals who were nearby. But there was also long-distance trade between some ancient empires. For instance, the Roman and Chinese empires were extremely far away, but they still traded with one another. They did this thanks to the Silk Road.

The Silk Road is the name of a trade route that started in China. It went across Asia to the Middle East. From there, it crossed the Mediterranean Sea and went to Rome. The Silk Road was not a single road though. It consisted of numerous routes. In fact, there were three major routes on the Silk Road. All three were difficult paths. Merchants had to travel through deserts and cross mountains and valleys. They sometimes even had to sail on water to get to their destinations. There were bandits and other dangers. But people wanted to trade for certain items, so merchants risked death to travel on the Silk Road.

Few people traveled the entire distance though. Most merchants only traded on small parts of the Silk Road. They bought and sold all kinds of goods. They traded spices, salt, tea, gold, and silk. Silk was the most highly desired item transported along the Silk Road. Because of it, many merchants became very wealthy.

Summary

Read the summary. Write the correct word(s) from the box in each blank. You may need to change the forms of the words.

dangerous	wealthy	silk	route	trade

Most people traded with individuals close to them. But there was some long-distance ________________ in the past. Rome and China traded on the Silk Road. The Silk Road was not one road. It was numerous ________________ that started in China and went across Asia and then to Rome. The Silk Road was ________________, but many merchants traded on it. They traded lots of goods, including ________________. A large number of merchants became ________________ from trading on the Silk Road.

Main Topic

Circle the correct answer.

1 What is the passage mainly about?

a. When people used the Silk Road

b. How people traveled on the Silk Road

c. What the Silk Road was

Details

Answer the questions.

2 Where did the Silk Road go?

a. From China to Rome

b. From China to Africa

c. From China to Russia

3 Which statement about the Silk Road is NOT correct?

a. It was often dangerous for merchants.

b. Most merchants traveled the entire Silk Road.

c. Merchants had to cross deserts and valleys.

4 What was the most desired item traded on the Silk Road?

a. Gold

b. Spices

c. Silk

5 Fill in the blank with the correct word(s).

The Silk Road was an example of long-distance trade between the ______________ and Chinese empires.

Vocabulary

Match the words and phrases with their definitions.

6	wealthy	a. a trader; a person who buys and sells products
7	risk death	b. a road; a route; a way
8	path	c. a low area between two or more mountains
9	merchant	d. rich
10	valley	e. to put one's life in danger

Reading Skills Practice: Cause and Effect I

What is cause and effect?

Use cause and effect to explain why something happens and the result of that action. The cause explains the reason that something occurs. Many times, the word *because* or *since* can explain the cause. The reason tells the result. Often, the word *so* or *therefore* explains the reason.

A **Read the passage again. Then, match each cause with its effect.**

a. People wanted to trade items,	i. they became wealthy.
b. Because many merchants sold silk,	ii. they have items that other people want.
c. People trade with others because	iii. so merchants risked their lives on the Silk Road.

B **Read another passage related to the topic and answer the questions.**

In the 1600s and 1700s, England had many colonies in North America. The people in the colonies were eager to trade. So a trading system developed. It was called Triangle Trade. It involved England, Africa, and the American colonies. Ships left England and went to Africa. They carried items like beads, weapons, and cloth. They traded them for African slaves. The slaves were loaded onto other ships. Those ships sailed to America. The American colonists needed many people to work on their plantations. So they bought the slaves that arrived on the ships. That was the second part of Triangle Trade. The third part involved shipping raw materials to England. Because England had many factories, it needed lots of raw materials to make finished products. So the colonists shipped sugar, tobacco, cotton, wood, and other goods to England.

1 Find the causes in the passage and underline them. Then, find the effects in the passage and circle them.

2 What did the American colonists ship to England?

a. Raw materials

b. Slaves

c. Finished products

3 Circle the correct word in each sentence.

a. England had many factories, (because / so) it needed a lot of raw materials.

b. (Because / So) the colonists wanted to trade, a trading system developed.

c. (Since / Therefore) the colonists needed workers, they bought African slaves.

UNIT 14 Bartering

Pre-Reading Questions

Answer the following questions.

1 What does the picture show?

2 Why do people barter?

3 Have you ever bartered for something? What was it?

4 What is your opinion of bartering?

Vocabulary

Write the correct word or phrase from the box for each definition.

civilization	agree	lack	service	worthless	poor

1 ____________ an activity that helps someone

2 ____________ not to have

3 ____________ bad; low

4 ____________ human society

5 ____________ to have the same opinion; to say yes to

6 ____________ having no value; worth nothing

Bartering

Track 14

Thousands of years ago, there was no money. But people often wanted to trade their items for ones that other people had. For example, perhaps a farmer had some potatoes. But he wanted some chickens that another farmer had. The farmer then offered a few potatoes for one chicken. If the other farmer agreed, they traded. Or perhaps one man needed his house repaired. So another man fixed his house in return for some food. These types of trades are known as bartering.

People barter by trading goods and services for other goods and services. There is no money involved. So people have to determine the values of their goods and the ones they want. Then, they can determine how to make trades for certain items.

People bartered for thousands of years. Even after money was invented, they still bartered. They did this for several reasons. For instance, some people lacked money. But they had goods to trade. So they traded their goods for other ones. Other times, bartering was more convenient than using money. For example, people who lived far away from civilization had no need for money. It had no value to them. So they just bartered for the goods and services they needed. Finally, at times, some countries' economies were poor. In those situations, their currencies were worthless. Because their money had no value, people bartered instead of using it to make purchases.

Summary

Read the summary. Write the correct word(s) from the box in each blank. You may need to change the forms of the words.

trading	economy	lack	service	money

In the past, there was no money, so people bartered for the goods and ________________ they needed. Bartering involves ________________ certain items for others. Even after money was invented, people continued to barter. Some of these people ________________ money, but they had goods and services to trade. Other people did not have a use for ________________. And some people lived in countries with poor ________________. Their money was worthless, so they had to barter.

Main Topic

Circle the correct answer.

1 What is the main topic of the passage?

a. The best ways to barter

b. The reasons that people barter

c. The importance of bartering

Details

Answer the questions.

2 What is bartering?

a. Trading goods and services for money

b. Trading goods and services for other goods and services

c. Trading goods and services for gold and silver

3 Which is NOT a reason that people bartered?

a. They did not want to pay taxes.

b. They did not have any money.

c. Their money was worthless.

4 Where do some people who barter live?

a. In big cities

b. In towns

c. Far from civilization

5 Fill in the blank with the correct word(s).

People who barter trade goods and services and do not use any ______________.

Vocabulary

Match the words and phrases with their definitions.

6	determine	a. a price; the amount that something is worth
7	currency	b. money
8	trade	c. to buy something
9	make a purchase	d. to decide
10	value	e. to exchange one thing for another

Reading Skills Practice: Cause and Effect II

What is cause and effect?
Use cause and effect to explain why something happens and the result of that action. The cause explains the reason that something occurs. The reason tells the result. The cause and effect may appear in the same sentence. Or they may appear in two different sentences. Pay close attention to find both of them.

A **Read the passage again. Then, match each cause with its effect.**

a. Money has no value to some people,	i. so they prefer to barter.
b. Because some people lack money,	ii. he trades some potatoes for it.
c. Since a farmer wants a chicken,	iii. they trade for goods and services.

B **Read another passage related to the topic and answer the questions.**

Dear Diary,

Today at school, we learned about money. Most countries use paper bills and coins as money nowadays. But it was different in the past. Societies used different objects as money. Many cultures valued metals like gold and silver. So they made gold and silver coins and used them as money. But some cultures did not have any gold or silver. So they found other items and used them as money. In Roman times, the army sometimes paid soldiers with salt. It was actually much more valuable than money, so the soldiers did not mind being paid that way. In the Netherlands a few centuries ago, people used tulip bulbs as money. And some ancient tribes used giant rocks or shells as money. Since the rocks and shells were rare, the tribes thought that they were worth a lot.

1 Find the causes in the passage and underline them. Then, find the effects in the passage and circle them.

2 What was used as money in the Netherlands a long time ago?

a. Shells

b. Salt

c. Tulip bulbs

3 Circle the correct word in each sentence.

a. (So / Because) rocks and shells were rare, they were valuable to the ancient tribes.

b. Salt was more valuable than money. (Therefore / Since) the soldiers did not mind getting paid with it.

c. Gold and silver were valuable, (so / since) people made coins with them.

UNIT 15

Franchises

Pre-Reading Questions

Answer the following questions.

1 What is a franchise?

2 What are some franchises that you know?

3 What do you think of franchises?

4 What are some advantages to franchises? What are some disadvantages?

Vocabulary

Write the correct word or phrase from the box for each definition.

right	train	spread	entire	highly	supply

1 ____________ to provide

2 ____________ permission; the legal ability to do something

3 ____________ complete; total

4 ____________ to educate; to teach

5 ____________ very

6 ____________ to expand; to go to other places

Franchises

Track 15

In cities and towns around the world, there are often similar sights. People may eat their meals at McDonald's or Burger King. They may get their coffee from Starbucks. And they may spend the night at the Hilton Hotel. All of these businesses are franchises.

A franchise gives a person the right to sell a product or service that belongs to another company. There are many kinds of franchises. Fast-food restaurants are the best-known ones. But they are not the only franchises. Hotels and delivery services are also often franchises. So are car dealerships and supermarkets.

There are many advantages to owning a franchise. First of all, the owner gets to operate a proven business model. This is very helpful for people who have never run a business before. In addition, the company that owns the franchise often trains the new employees. It also provides other assistance. For instance, fast-food restaurants supply their franchises with food. And coffee shop companies supply their franchises with coffee.

The first franchises began in the 1800s. But they did not become popular until the 1950s. That was when McDonald's started to open many restaurants. Since then, franchises have spread around the world. Many of them are highly successful.

Thanks to franchises, many people are able to go into business for themselves. But, due to their support network, they are not in business alone. They have entire companies that look after them.

Summary

Read the summary. Write the correct word from the box in each blank. You may need to change the forms of the words.

support	owner	service	advantage	restaurant

Many cities and towns around the world have franchises. A franchise is the right for someone to sell a good or ____________ belonging to another company. A lot of fast-food ____________ are franchises. But other businesses have franchises, too. Franchises have several ____________. They are good for first-time business ____________. The companies provide ____________ in many ways. Franchises started in the 1800s and have spread around the world today. A lot of them are highly successful companies.

Main Topic

Circle the correct answer.

1 What is the passage mainly about?
  a. Why people like to run franchises
  b. The world's most popular franchises
  c. Fast-food franchises

Details

Answer the questions.

2 What are the best-known franchises?
  a. Delivery services
  b. Fast-food restaurants
  c. Supermarkets

3 Which is NOT an advantage of owning a franchise?
  a. The company trains the new workers.
  b. The owner always makes a profit.
  c. The owner gets a proven business model.

4 When did McDonald's start to open many restaurants?
  a. The 1800s
  b. The 1920s
  c. The 1950s

5 Fill in the blank with the correct word(s).

> Franchises provide a support network for people who go into ________________ for themselves.

Vocabulary

Match the words and phrases with their definitions.

6	support network	a. to take care of; to protect; to help
7	car dealership	b. a good point; a benefit
8	look after	c. a group that provides help for others
9	proven	d. a business that sells cars
10	advantage	e. successful; known to work

Reading Skills Practice: Identifying Cohesive Devices I

A Read the passage again. Then, circle the correct words.

a. The owner gets a proven business model. (In addition / Because), the company trains the new employees.

b. Fast-food restaurants are well-known franchises. (Therefore / However) there are other kinds of franchises, too.

c. Franchises became popular in the 1950s (when / why) McDonald's began to open many restaurants.

What is identifying cohesive devices?
Use identifying cohesive devices to make a passage read better. Many cohesive devices are conjunctions as well as other connecting words. Some of these words are *and*, *but*, *because*, *while*, *in addition*, and *finally*. By using these words, you can show the relationships between various actions, causes and effects, and events in a passage.

B Read another passage related to the topic and answer the questions.

In 1940, two brothers, Richard and Maurice McDonald, opened a restaurant in San Bernardino, California. They called it McDonald's. They wanted to become rich. So they worked very hard. They also developed a new system for preparing food. It was based on the assembly line. As a result, they could prepare food very quickly. Then, in 1954, Ray Kroc began to work with the McDonald brothers. He realized the potential of the restaurant. So he wanted to expand it around the world. But the brothers did not want to expand quickly. So Kroc purchased the rights to the restaurant from the McDonald brothers. Kroc made them rich, but he became the owner. Then, he opened franchises in the United States. In addition, McDonald's franchises started opening in other countries. Today, there are more than 34,000 McDonald's franchises in 119 countries.

1 Find the connecting words in the passage and circle them.

2 What did Ray Kroc do?

a. He introduced an assembly line system to McDonald's.

b. He opened 34,000 restaurants all around the world.

c. He purchased the rights to the McDonald's franchise.

3 Choose the correct connecting words for the sentences.

a. McDonald's franchises opened in the United States. They (in addition / also) opened around the world.

b. The two brothers wanted to become rich, (so / or) they worked very hard.

c. Ray Kroc wanted to open many franchises quickly, (and / but) the brothers wanted to open them slowly.

UNIT 16 Changes in the U.S. Dollar

Pre-Reading Questions

Answer the following questions.

1 What kinds of money can you see in the pictures?

2 Have you ever had any U.S. dollars? Why did you have them?

3 What money is used in your country?

4 Do you know the names of the money used in other countries? What are they?

Vocabulary

Write the correct word or phrase from the box for each definition.

counterfeit	bill	recognized	prepare	value	coming

1 ____________ familiar; known

2 ____________ approaching; in the future

3 ____________ paper money

4 ____________ to make something that is fake or not real

5 ____________ worth; the price of something

6 ____________ to get ready

Changes in the U.S. Dollar

Track 16

The U.S. dollar is used in the United States. It is also accepted in many other countries around the world. In addition, a lot of international business is done with the U.S. dollar. It is the most recognized type of money in the world today. But the dollar did not always look like it does today. In fact, it has changed a lot over the years.

For instance, the first dollars were printed in America in 1690. At that time, the United States was not even a country. These dollars were printed by the Massachusetts Bay Colony. Later, other colonies printed their own money as well.

Decades later in the 1700s, the colonists were preparing for war with England. To pay for the coming war, they began to make their own money. The colonists printed money called Continental Currency in 1775. But these dollars were easy to counterfeit. And they often had little or no value.

The first real American dollars were printed in 1785. They looked very different from the dollars used today. The reason is that the designs of the bills often changed. For instance, the first ten-dollar bills had the image of Abraham Lincoln. Later, Andrew Jackson's picture was on the ten-dollar bill. Today, Alexander Hamilton's image is on it. The pictures on the fronts of other U.S. dollars have changed in similar ways. And other pictures and designs on the bills have undergone many alterations as well.

Summary

Read the summary. Write the correct word(s) from the box in each blank. You may need to change the forms of the words.

print	colonist	bill	world	design

The U.S. dollar is used around the ______________, and many people recognize it. But it has not always looked like it does today. The first dollars were ______________ by the Massachusetts Bay Colony in 1690. The American ______________ also printed Continental Currency in 1775. But the first real American dollars were printed in 1785. Since then, the ______________ of the dollar has changed a lot. For instance, the images on the ten-dollar ______________ have changed frequently.

Main Topic

Circle the correct answer.

1 What is the main topic of the passage?

a. The changing value of the U.S. dollar

b. The changes in who prints U.S. dollars

c. How the U.S. dollar has changed over time

Details

Answer the questions.

2 When was the first money printed in America?

a. 1690

b. 1775

c. 1785

3 Which statement about Continental Currency is true?

a. It was hard for people to counterfeit.

b. It was printed in England.

c. It often had a very low value.

4 Which person's image has NOT been on the ten-dollar bill?

a. George Washington

b. Alexander Hamilton

c. Abraham Lincoln

5 Fill in the blank with the correct word(s).

The design of the U.S. dollar has often ________________, so the money has had many different appearances.

Vocabulary

Match the words and phrases with their definitions.

6	print money	a. a picture
7	image	b. between two or more countries
8	be accepted	c. to make money
9	alteration	d. a change
10	international	e. to be used; to be legal

Reading Skills Practice: Identifying Cohesive Devices II

A Read the passage again. Then, choose what it refers to.

> For instance, the first ten-dollar bills had the image of Abraham Lincoln. Later, Andrew Jackson's picture was on the ten-dollar bill. Today, Alexander Hamilton's image is on it.

a. Andrew Jackson's picture

b. the ten-dollar bill

c. Alexander Hamilton's image

What is identifying cohesive devices?

Use identifying cohesive devices to make a passage read better. Many cohesive devices are pronouns. Some of them are words such as *he*, *she*, *it*, *this*, and *that*. By using pronouns, you do not have to repeat nouns throughout the passage. Pronouns can improve the quality of the writing in a passage. Be sure to know which nouns the pronouns refer to.

B Read another passage related to the topic and answer the questions.

Dear Sally,

I just arrived in the United States. I am looking forward to studying here. The country is nice, but the money can be very confusing. There are several types of bills and coins. The bills are easy to use. However, the coins are confusing because they all have names. And many Americans use the names of the coins instead of their values. For instance, a one-cent coin is called a penny. A five-cent coin is a nickel. A ten-cent coin is a dime. And a twenty-five-cent coin is a quarter. They even have fifty-cent coins and dollar coins. But those coins lack special names. I need to remember the names of the coins to make my time here more comfortable. I forgot them the last time I went shopping. So I was a little embarrassed.

Your friend,
Julie

1 Find the pronouns in the passage and circle them.

2 What is the name of a twenty-five-cent coin?

a. A quarter

b. A nickel

c. A dime

3 Read the passage again. Then, choose what they refers to.

a. the bills

b. the coins

c. names

Chapter

5

Ancient Societies

UNIT 17 Ancient Egypt

Pre-Reading Questions

Answer the following questions.

1 What can you see in the picture?

2 How important was the Nile River to ancient Egypt?

3 Who were some pharaohs in ancient Egypt?

4 What do you know about ancient Egypt?

Vocabulary

Write the correct word or phrase from the box for each definition.

flow	arise	farm	source	neighboring	pharaoh

1 ____________ to move as a liquid

2 ____________ to grow crops on land

3 ____________ a king of Egypt

4 ____________ nearby; close

5 ____________ to start; to begin

6 ____________ an origin; the place where something begins

Ancient Egypt

Track 17

The source of the Nile River is in Central Africa. The river flows north from there all the way to the Mediterranean Sea. On the last part of its journey, it goes through Egypt. Much of the land in Egypt is desert, but the Nile is so powerful that it flows through that barren land.

Humans began living in Egypt more than 100,000 years ago. They were able to survive there thanks to the Nile. Around 10,000 years ago, people started to farm the land by the Nile. Thanks to the river's annual floods, the land near the Nile is very fertile. It was beside the Nile that one of the greatest of all ancient civilizations arose: Egypt.

Around 3,200 B.C., ancient Egypt was united under one kingdom. For nearly 3,000 years afterward, pharaohs then ruled the land. The Egyptian pharaohs were kings. But the Egyptians considered them to be like gods. Some of the pharaohs were great men. They included Narmer, Ramses the Great, and Amenhotep. Because of these pharaohs and others, Egypt became a powerful empire. Egyptians armies conquered neighboring lands, and Egypt was the strongest empire in Africa and the Middle East for centuries.

The Egyptians were also great builders. They constructed numerous pyramids all over the land. They also made the Great Sphinx. Many of their monuments and other buildings remain standing today. They allow modern-day people to see how great Egypt once was.

Summary

Read the summary. Write the correct word(s) from the box in each blank. You may need to change the forms of the words.

god	monument	powerful	civilization	pharaoh

The Nile River flows through Egypt on its way to the Mediterranean Sea. Thanks to the Nile, an ancient ______________ arose in Egypt thousands of years ago. The ______________ ruled Egypt for nearly 3,000 years. They were like ______________ to the Egyptians. Under the pharaohs, Egypt became the most ______________ empire in Africa and the Middle East. The Egyptians constructed numerous pyramids and ______________. Today, people can still see many of them.

Main Topic

Circle the correct answer.

1 What is the main topic of the passage?

a. The greatest Egyptian pharaohs

b. Ancient Egyptian civilization

c. The course of the Nile River

Details

Answer the questions.

2 Where is the source of the Nile River?

a. The Mediterranean Sea

b. Central Africa

c. Egypt

3 For how long did the pharaohs rule Egypt?

a. Around 3,000 years

b. Around 10,000 years

c. Around 100,000 years

4 Which is NOT true about the pharaohs?

a. The Egyptian people considered them to be gods.

b. They helped Egypt become a powerful empire.

c. They conquered Africa and the entire Middle East.

5 Fill in the blank with the correct word(s).

The Egyptians built many ______________ and monuments throughout the land.

Vocabulary

Match the words and phrases with their definitions.

6	monument	a. empty; unproductive; dead
7	barren	b. yearly; happening every year
8	thanks to	c. a building made in honor of a person or event
9	annual	d. because of
10	fertile	e. productive; rich

Reading Skills Practice: Outlining I

What is outlining?
Use outlining to summarize the main points of a passage. Use short phrases in your outline. Start by noting the main idea or action in a paragraph. Then, write down the main details in the paragraph. A paragraph may have one, two, three, or more main details.

A Read the passage again. Then, complete the outline by writing the correct words.

Ancient Egypt

I. Humans lived in Egypt thanks to the a.______________
  i. Has annual b.______________, so the land near it is fertile

II. Egypt was united under one kingdom in 3,200 B.C.
  i. Was ruled by c.______________ for 3,000 years
  ii. Were kings but were considered gods
  iii. Included Narmer, Ramses the Great, and Amenhotep

III. Egypt became a powerful d.______________ in Africa and the Middle East

IV. Egyptians were great builders
  i. e.______________ pyramids, the Great Sphinx, and other monuments
  ii. Can still see many today

B Read another passage related to the topic and answer the questions.

Most ancient societies grew up around rivers. They did this for a few reasons. First, the rivers provided drinking water. They let people farm the land. They were sources of food when people learned to fish. And people could easily transport goods on rivers. One early human civilization arose by two rivers. They were the Tigris and Euphrates. This area was called Mesopotamia. It means "the place between two rivers."

The first human cities were founded in Mesopotamia. Over a period of centuries, several empires formed there. Two were the Sumerian and Babylonian empires. They both helped human civilization develop. For instance, the Sumerians invented one of the first writing systems. They also made their own form of government. And the Babylonians were the first people to write down their laws. These and other advances let human society progress.

1 Complete the outline by filling in the blanks.

Mesopotamia

I. Is located by the a.______________ and Euphrates rivers
  i. Means "the place between two rivers"

II. First human b.______________ founded there

III. c.______________ were one empire
  i. Invented a d.______________ system
  ii. Made their own form of government

IV. Babylonians were another empire
  i. Were the first people to write down e.______________

2 What did the Babylonians do?

a. They invented writing.

b. They wrote down their laws.

c. They made the first government.

UNIT 18

The Chinese Qin Dynasty

Pre-Reading Questions

Answer the following questions.

1 What can you see in the picture?

2 Where do you think these statues were found?

3 When was the Qin Dynasty?

4 What do you know about ancient China?

Vocabulary

Write the correct word or phrase from the box for each definition.

kingdom	protect	measure	chariot	declare	dynasty

1 ______________ to guard; to keep safe

2 ______________ a group of rulers from the same family

3 ______________ a vehicle with two wheels that is pulled by horses

4 ______________ a system of determining the size and length of objects

5 ______________ a land that is ruled by a king

6 ______________ to announce; to state

The Chinese Qin Dynasty

Track 18

In ancient China, there were many kingdoms. They often fought one another. Then, in 221 B.C., Qin Shi Huangdi defeated all of these kingdoms and unified China. Then, he declared himself to be the emperor of China. He was the founder of the Qin Dynasty.

The Qin Dynasty only lasted for a short time. However, it was one of the most important dynasties in Chinese history. As emperor, Qin Shi Huangdi made China larger than it had ever been before. He also began many construction projects. He had roads built all throughout his empire. He also did a great amount of work on the Great Wall of China. He wanted the wall to be strong to protect China from foreign enemies.

Qin Shi Huangdi wanted to show that China was a unified country. So he made an effort to standardize the writing people used throughout China. He wanted everyone to write the same way. He also standardized the laws, weights, measures, and currency.

When he died, Qin Shi Huangdi was buried in an enormous tomb. It was hidden for more than 2,000 years. Then, in 1974, some farmers digging in a field near Xian accidently found his tomb. Inside the tomb were thousands of terracotta warriors. The emperor had been buried with an entire army of life-sized statues. There were soldiers, horses, and chariots. The tomb of Emperor Qin Shi Huangdi is one of the greatest archaeological discoveries in history.

Summary

Read the summary. Write the correct word(s) from the box in each blank. You may need to change the forms of the words.

currency	tomb	dynasty	construction	emperor

In 221 B.C., Qin Shi Huangdi united China and founded the Qin Dynasty. The ______________ did not last long, but it was very important to China. China became larger than ever. There were many road ______________ projects, and work was done on the Great Wall of China. Qin Shi Huangdi also standardized writing, laws, weights, measures, and ______________. When the ______________ died, he was buried near Xian with an army of terracotta warriors. His ______________ was discovered in 1974.

Main Topic

Circle the correct answer.

1 What is the passage mainly about?

a. The unification of China

b. The greatest dynasty in ancient China

c. The Emperor Qin Shi Huangdi

Details

Answer the questions.

2 Which is NOT true about Qin Shi Huangdi?

a. He built the first roads in China.

b. He did work on the Great Wall of China.

c. He was the founder of the Qin Dynasty.

3 What did Qin Shi Huangdi standardize?

a. Education

b. Laws

c. Spoken language

4 What was found near Xian in 1974?

a. The palace of Qin Shi Huangdi

b. The birthplace of Qin Shi Huangdi

c. The tomb of Qin Shi Huangdi

5 Fill in the blank with the correct word(s).

The army of terracotta ________________ is one of the greatest archaeological discoveries in history.

Vocabulary

Match the words and phrases with their definitions.

6	tomb	a. to make the same everywhere
7	standardize	b. the person who starts something
8	life-sized	c. a clay statue of a soldier
9	founder	d. a grave; the place where someone is buried
10	terracotta warrior	e. actual sized

Reading Skills Practice: Outlining II

What is outlining?
Use outlining to summarize the main points of a passage. Use short phrases in your outline. Start by noting the main idea or action in a paragraph. Then, write down the main details in the paragraph. Do not write down the minor details in the paragraph. You only need to focus on the main details.

A Read the passage again. Then, complete the outline by writing the correct words.

The Qin Dynasty

I. Was founded by Qin Shi Huangdi in 221 B.C.
   i. Defeated other kingdoms and a.____________ China
II. Was important b.____________
   i. China became larger than ever
   ii. Did construction work on roads and the Great Wall of China
   iii. Standardized c.____________, laws, weights, measures, and currency
III. Emperor was buried in enormous d.____________ when died
   i. Was hidden for more than 2,000 years
IV. Tomb was found near Xian in 1974
   i. Contained thousands of e.____________ warriors
   ii. Were life-sized f.____________ of soldiers, horses, and chariots
   iii. Was a great archaeological discovery

B Read another passage related to the topic and answer the questions.

Dear Diary,

I returned from my trip to China last night. I visited many places there. But the most impressive site was the Great Wall of China. Before I went to China, I had thought that the Great Wall was just one long wall. But that is not true. It is a large number of different walls. The Chinese started making it around 2,500 years ago. They built it to protect themselves from invaders from the north. The Great Wall stretches more than 7,000 kilometers. I visited the wall with my tour group, and we walked along a small part of it. I could not believe how large it is. It was an amazing act of engineering for the Chinese to build it. Of course, they did not build it in just a few years. They worked on it for hundreds of years.

1 Complete the outline by filling in the blanks.

The Great Wall of China

I. Is a large number of different walls
II. Chinese started making it a.____________ years ago
   i. Was for protection from northern b.____________
III. Stretches more than c.____________ kilometers
IV. Was an amazing act of d.____________
   i. Was not built in a few years
   ii. Took e.____________ of years to make

2 How long is the Great Wall of China?

a. Hundreds of kilometers

b. Around 2,500 kilometers

c. More than 7,000 kilometers

UNIT 19

Harappan Civilization

Pre-Reading Questions

Answer the following questions.

1 What is this picture of?

2 Where was the Harappan Civilization located?

3 How old do you think it was?

4 What do you know about ancient cultures in your country?

Vocabulary

Write the correct word or phrase from the box for each definition.

severe	bronze	hieroglyphics	relic	vanish	collapse

1 ____________ a metal that is a combination of copper and tin

2 ____________ an object that was made in the past

3 ____________ serious

4 ____________ a writing system that uses pictures as words

5 ____________ to fall; to end

6 ____________ to disappear

Harappan Civilization

Track 19

There were many human societies in the past. Most of them vanished without a trace. Others left ruins and relics. The ruins are from buildings such as temples and palaces. The relics include pieces of pottery, weapons, and jewelry. Archaeologists study all of these things to learn about past societies. Yet archaeologists do not learn everything since there are still many mysteries about civilizations from ancient times.

This is true about the Harappan Civilization. The Harappan people lived in the Indus River Valley. Their society was located where Pakistan and India are today. It was one of the four great ancient civilizations. The other three were in Egypt, Mesopotamia, and China. The Harappan Civilization began around 3300 B.C. And it lasted until about 2000 B.C. The Harappan people had an urban culture. They used a grid system to make their cities. They built stone houses. They had sewage systems. They made tools and weapons with bronze. They even had their own writing system. They used hieroglyphics. So they based their writing on pictures rather than words.

Archaeologists have learned a lot by studying Harappan culture. But they have been unable to learn one thing: why Harappan society ended. Around 2000 B.C., Harappan society collapsed. Some experts think a severe drought took place. So there was not enough water. Others believe invaders killed the Harappan people. No one knows for sure. Sadly, archaeologists may never learn why the Harappan Civilization fell.

Summary

Read the summary. Write the correct word(s) from the box in each blank. You may need to change the forms of the words.

trace	tool	society	mysterious	drought

A lot of ancient civilizations vanished without a ______________. Others left ruins and relics that archaeologists study. The Harappan Civilization is ______________. It existed in the Indus River Valley from around 3300 B.C. to 2000 B.C. The Harappan people built cities with a grid system. They made bronze ______________ and wrote with hieroglyphics. But Harappan ______________ suddenly collapsed around 2000 B.C. Archaeologists are not sure why. There may have been a severe ______________. Or invaders may have killed them.

Main Topic

Circle the correct answer.

1 What is the passage mainly about?

a. Facts about the Harappan Civilization

b. The greatest achievements of the Harappan people

c. The location of the Harappan Civilization

Details

Answer the questions.

2 Which of the following is a relic?

a. A palace

b. A temple

c. A piece of pottery

3 What kind of culture did the Harappan people have?

a. An urban culture

b. A farming culture

c. A fishing culture

4 Which is NOT a reason that the Harappan Civilization may have disappeared?

a. Invaders killed all of the people.

b. An earthquake killed everyone.

c. There was a severe drought.

5 Fill in the blank with the correct word(s).

Archaeologists study ________________ and relics to learn about cultures from the past.

Vocabulary

Match the words and phrases with their definitions.

6	sewage system	a. a long period of time with little or no rain
7	without a trace	b. a group of straight lines that intersect at right angles
8	drought	c. a system that removes human waste
9	fall	d. to end
10	grid system	e. without leaving anything behind

Reading Skills Practice: Simplifying I

What is simplifying?
Use simplifying to make long sentences shorter. Sometimes a sentence may be very long. It might have two, three, or four parts. To simplify the sentence, identify the main details in the sentence. Then, remove the other information. By simplifying, you can remove unnecessary words and make long sentences much shorter.

A Read the passage again. Then, look at the sentence below. Choose the answer choice that best simplifies the sentence.

> Yet archaeologists do not learn everything since there are still many mysteries about civilizations from ancient times.

a. Archaeologists know all about mysteries from ancient civilizations.
b. There are some civilizations that archaeologists know everything about.
c. Archaeologists still have not solved some mysteries from the past.

B Read another passage related to the topic and answer the questions.

The Harappan people had their own religion. They worshipped many gods. After the Harappan Civilization fell, a new group of people settled in India. They had their own gods. But these new people also took some of the Harappan gods and made them their own. Centuries later, Hinduism developed. The *Rig Veda* is the earliest known writing about Hinduism. It was probably created around 1000 B.C. But it was not written down until about 300 B.C. Before then, people either sang or spoke it. Hinduism was a polytheistic religion. So it had a large number of gods. Vishnu and Shiva were two of the most important Hindu gods, but there were many others. They included Indra, Ganesha, Kali, and Krishna. Over the years, Hinduism became the dominant religion in India. Today, millions of people around the world practice it.

1 Find the sentences in the passage with two or more parts and underline them.

2 What was the *Rig Veda*?
a. A work by the Harappan people
b. An ancient work about Hinduism
c. A modern-day work about Hinduism

3 Look at the sentence below. Then, choose the answer choice that best simplifies the sentence.

> Vishnu and Shiva were two of the most important Hindu gods, but there were many others.

a. Vishnu and Shiva were important, but there was other Hindu gods.
b. All of the Hindu gods, including Vishnu and Shiva, were important.
c. There were just two gods in Hinduism: Vishnu and Shiva.

UNIT **20**

The Aztec Empire

Pre-Reading Questions

Answer the following questions.

1 What are the people in the picture wearing?

2 Where was the Aztec Empire located?

3 What else do you know about the Aztec Empire?

4 Do you know about any other groups of people in the Americas?

Vocabulary

Write the correct word or phrase from the box for each definition.

establish	warlike	eager	nomadic	battle	ally

1 ____________ wanting to fight

2 ____________ wandering; roaming

3 ____________ a friend; a partner

4 ____________ willing to do something

5 ____________ to found; to create; to make

6 ____________ to fight; to make war against

The Aztec Empire

Track 20

In the 1300s, a nomadic group of people in Central America settled down on some islands in Lake Texcoco. They built a city and called it Tenochtitlan. As time passed, they established one of the greatest empires in the Americas. These were the Aztec people. And they founded the Aztec Empire.

Tenochtitlan was located on the site of modern-day Mexico City. It served as the power base of the Aztec people. They were a very warlike group. During the 1400s and 1500s, they fought many battles with neighboring tribes. They usually defeated these tribes. As they won these wars, the Aztecs were able to expand the size of their empire.

Most of the tribes that lived near the Aztecs feared them because the Aztecs often tried to capture the warriors that they fought battles with. Then, the Aztecs took their prisoners back to Tenochtitlan. There, they held religious ceremonies. At these events, the Aztecs prayed to their gods. Then, they performed human sacrifices for their gods. So the Aztecs killed all of their prisoners.

The Spanish arrived in Aztec territory in 1519. They were led by Hernan Cortez. He wanted to fight the Aztecs. The nearby tribes were eager to help him. From 1519 to 1521, the Spanish and their native allies battled the Aztecs. Finally, they captured Tenochtitlan and won the war. The Spanish then became the new masters of the region.

Summary

Read the summary. Write the correct word(s) from the box in each blank. You may need to change the forms of the words.

religious	defeat	expand	tribe	fear

The Aztecs built a city called Tenochtitlan and founded the Aztec Empire. Tenochtitlan was the Aztecs' power base. In the 1400s and 1500s, they won many wars and ________________ the size of their empire. The neighboring tribes ________________ the Aztecs. The reason was that the Aztecs took prisoners and then killed them during ________________ ceremonies. When the Spanish arrived in 1519, the nearby ________________ joined them to fight the Aztecs. In 1521, the Spanish ________________ the Aztec Empire.

Main Topic

Circle the correct answer.

1 What is the main topic of the passage?

a. The defeat of the Aztecs by the Spanish
b. The tribes that lived in Central America
c. The characteristics of the Aztec Empire

Details

Answer the questions.

2 What was Tenochtitlan?

a. The capital of the Aztec Empire
b. The capital of Central America
c. The capital of the Spanish Empire

3 How did the Aztecs expand the size of their empire?

a. By buying land from other tribes
b. By farming land no one lived on
c. By winning wars against other tribes

4 Which statement about the Aztecs is NOT true?

a. They killed captured warriors in religious ceremonies.
b. The neighboring tribes all liked the Aztecs.
c. They were defeated in battle by the Spanish.

5 Fill in the blank with the correct word(s).

Hernan Cortez led the ________________ to victory in a war against the Aztecs.

Vocabulary

Match the words and phrases with their definitions.

6 religious ceremony	•	• a. the act of killing a person during a special service
7 power base	•	• b. land belonging to someone
8 human sacrifice	•	• c. to move to an area and to live there
9 territory	•	• d. an area where a group is very strong
10 settle down	•	• e. a service done when one worships a god or gods

Reading Skills Practice: Simplifying II

What is simplifying?
Use simplifying to make long sentences shorter. Sometimes a sentence may be very long. It might have two, three, or four parts. To simplify the sentence, identify the main details in the sentence. Then, remove the other information. Be sure to ignore the minor details in the sentence. Only the main details are important.

A **Read the passage again. Then, look at the sentence below. Choose the answer choice that best simplifies the sentence.**

> Most of the tribes that lived near the Aztecs feared them because the Aztecs often tried to capture the warriors that they fought battles with.

a. The tribes that lived near the Aztecs fought them and often captured many Aztec warriors.
b. The Aztecs tried to capture warriors in battle, so the tribes that lived near the Aztecs feared them.
c. During battles, the Aztecs captured many warriors because they were too scared to fight.

B **Read another passage related to the topic and answer the questions.**

Dear Kelly,

I am still on vacation in Mexico, and I am visiting a lot of ancient sites. They are so fascinating. The other day, I visited a place called Chichen Itza. It used to be a large city. But today there are only ruins. It was a city that was built by the Mayans. The Mayan Empire existed in Central America many centuries ago. The Mayans were powerful from around the years 600 to 1200. Can you imagine that? They had a great civilization in the rainforests of Central America for at least 600 years. That is incredible. Then, something happened to the Mayans. No one is exactly sure what happened, but Mayan society suddenly became weak, so the Mayan Empire collapsed. I wonder what took place. It must have been a bad event.

Your friend,
Alice

1 Find the sentences in the passage with two or more parts and underline them.

2 Who built Chichen Itza?

a. The Aztecs b. The Mexicans c. The Mayans

3 Look at the sentence below. Then, choose the answer choice that best simplifies the sentence.

> No one is exactly sure what happened, but Mayan society suddenly became weak, so the Mayan Empire collapsed.

a. Mayan society was so weak that the Mayan Empire collapsed.
b. The Mayan Empire disappeared for several reasons.
c. For some reason, the Mayan Empire lost power and then fell.

Answers

Answers

Chapter 1 Weather

Unit 01 | Hurricanes

p. 11

Pre-Reading Questions Sample Answer

1 It looks like a bad storm. I think the water is going onto the land.
2 No, there are not. But my country gets typhoons every year. They are similar storms.
3 There is a lot of rain and wind during a hurricane.
4 Yes, I have. I have been in many typhoons. They are not fun, especially if you are outside. They can be dangerous because of their winds and heavy rains.

Vocabulary

1 crash　2 blow
3 landfall　4 inland
5 evaporate　6 massive

p. 12

Summary

Sometimes storms cause heavy rain and wind and bring a lot of water onto land. These storms are hurricanes. Hurricanes are tropical storms that form in areas with warm water. They begin as tropical storms. As their wind speeds increase, they become hurricanes. Some hurricanes have winds that blow more than 150 kilometers per hour and are nearly 1,000 kilometers across. Hurricanes that make landfall can cause flooding. This can damage buildings and kill people.

p. 13

Comprehension

1 b　2 c　3 a
4 b　5 hour

6 d　7 b　8 e
9 c　10 a

p. 14

Reading Skills Practice: Details I

A a. tropical storm. Atlantic Ocean
b. twenty-six, upward
c. wind speed, 119

B
1 People in Asia refer to tropical storms as typhoons. These are the same types of storms as hurricanes. People call tropical storms in the Atlantic Ocean and eastern Pacific Ocean hurricanes. They call tropical storms in the western Pacific Ocean typhoons. And those storms that occur in the Indian Ocean are cyclones. Yet they are all the same type of storm. Sadly, tropical storms are often responsible for large numbers of deaths. For instance, the deadliest storm in history took place in Bangladesh. It happened in 1970. Between half a million to one million people perished when a cyclone made landfall. In the 1700s and 1800s, there were several deadly typhoons and cyclones. A few killed several hundred thousand people each. In more recent times, a cyclone that hit Myanmar in 2008 killed at least 100,000 people.

2 c
3 a. F　b. T　c. F

Unit 02 | Tornadoes

p. 15

Pre-Reading Questions Sample Answer

1 It's like a wind funnel. The air moves really fast.
2 A tornado can destroy many houses and other buildings. It can be very dangerous.
3 No, it doesn't. So I think we're very lucky.
4 I think it would be very scary.

Vocabulary

1 extend　2 regrettably
3 destructive　4 twister
5 path　6 fairly

p. 16

Summary

Tornadoes are extremely <u>violent</u> and destructive forces of nature. They usually happen during thunderstorms. When warm air and hot air meet, the air might spin <u>rapidly</u>. This can form a tornado. Some tornadoes have winds that <u>blow</u> more than 500 kilometers per hour. Most tornadoes are thin, but some may <u>extend</u> for two or three kilometers. Tornado Alley is a place in the United States that gets many tornadoes. People in that <u>region</u> always watch out for tornadoes.

p. 17

Comprehension

1 a   2 c   3 b
4 a   5 United States

6 e   7 a   8 c
9 b   10 d

p. 18

Reading Skills Practice: Details II

A a. warm, cold
b. spin, winds
c. Tornado Alley, spring

B

Dear Diary,

Last night was the most frightening moment of my life. Everyone in my family was watching TV in the living room. Suddenly, the power went out. A moment later, we heard sirens going off in the distance. Then, we heard a sound that was like the loudest freight train I had ever heard. My parents both yelled, "Tornado!" My brother and I didn't know what to do. <u>My parents made us go down to the basement and hide underneath the big table there. All four of us remained there until we couldn't hear the tornado anymore.</u> Then, we went upstairs. Our house was a mess. All of the windows were broken, and a tree had crashed through the roof. We went outside and saw it was even worse. Two of our neighbors' homes were totally destroyed. I couldn't believe my eyes.

2 a
3 a. T   b. F   c. T

Unit 03 | The Water Cycle

p. 19

Pre-Reading Questions Sample Answer

1 It's how water takes different forms. It shows how water is on the ground and in the air.
2 It is important because we can see the different stages that water exists in.
3 Most of the planet is covered with water. I think there's lots of water on the Earth.
4 Humans have to drink water, or they'll die. Plants and animals also need water in order to live.

Vocabulary

1 constant   2 condense
3 release   4 soak
5 unite   6 transform

p. 20

Summary

The water cycle has four stages. The first is evaporation. This happens when water in <u>oceans</u>, seas, rivers, and lakes becomes water vapor and rises into the air. Next is condensation. The water vapor turns into water droplets, which unite to form <u>clouds</u>. The third stage is precipitation. This happens when <u>rain</u>, snow, and other forms of water fall to the ground. The fourth stage is <u>collection</u>. The water returns to the surface, where it can <u>evaporate</u> again.

p. 21

Comprehension

1 a   2 b   3 b
4 c   5 four

6 e   7 a   8. c
9 b   10 d

p. 22

Reading Skills Practice: Connecting Words I

A a. But b. When c. In addition

B

1

On most days, people can look at the sky and see clouds in it. Clouds are collections of tiny drops of water and crystals of ice. There are many different types of clouds. People can predict the type of weather that will occur simply by looking at them. For instance, clouds that are very high in the atmosphere are cirrus clouds. These white clouds are often indicators of pleasant weather. Yet they are also signs that there may be rain by the next day. Alto clouds, on the other hand, are clouds at medium altitudes. These clouds may cover the entire sky. In addition, they often indicate either thunderstorms or the continual falling of rain and snow. The lowest clouds in the sky are stratus clouds. They may sometimes indicate light rain. However, no precipitation usually falls from them.

2 b

3 a. And b. Yet c. In addition

Unit 04 | Snow

p. 23

Pre-Reading Questions Sample Answer

1 In the first picture, there are many trees covered with snow. The scene looks nice. In the second picture, there is a lot of snow on a highway, so there is a traffic jam.

2 It snows several times each winter in my country.

3 Snow can cause traffic jams on streets. It can also knock down power lines, so people can lose electricity at their homes.

4 Snow is okay. I like to play in it. But I don't like a lot of snow.

Vocabulary

1 snowstorm 2 light

3 breathtaking 4 frozen

5 peak 6 impassable

p. 24

Summary

Snow can be both beautiful and deadly. Snow can fall when the temperature falls below zero degrees Celsius. Water in clouds turns into ice crystals, and these then fall to the ground as snow. Snow often falls in places with cold winters. Yet it can also fall in hot deserts and even in Hawaii at times. When snowfall is light, there are few problems. But heavy snowfall can result in many problems, including the deaths of people.

p. 25

Comprehension

1 c 2 b 3 c

4 b 5 breathtaking

6 c 7 e 8 b

9 a 10 d

p. 26

Reading Skills Practice: Connecting Words II

A a. but b. When c. and

B

1

Dear Gina,

I am having a great time in Switzerland. It is a beautiful country with lots of mountains. We have gone skiing a few times and mountain climbing once. That was a frightening experience because a blizzard happened then. Here is what happened: We were climbing a mountain when it started to snow. Our guide said it was not a problem, but he was wrong. Suddenly, the snow began falling heavily. We could not see a single thing. It was totally white. We were caught in a blizzard. Our guide yelled to us and told us not to move. I was so scared during the blizzard. Fortunately, it only lasted for around twenty minutes. When the blizzard ended, there was a lot of snow on the ground. I was really happy to get back to the hotel that day.

Your friend,
Mark

2 a

3 a. and b. so c. when

Chapter 2 Literature

Unit 05 | *The Jungle Book*

p. 29

Pre-Reading Questions Sample Answer

1 I see a boy with some wolves in one picture. And I see a boy, a wolf, a dead man, and a tiger in the other picture.

2 Monkeys and tigers live in the jungle. So do many snakes and insects.

3 Yes, I do, but it would be very difficult.

4 I think it would be scary. The jungle is very dangerous.

Vocabulary

1	immediate	2	influence
3	tale	4	publish
5	colony	6	obey

p. 30

Summary

Rudyard Kipling was a British writer who lived in India for many years. He wrote *The Jungle Book* in 1894. It was a collection of tales mostly about Mowgli, a boy who grew up in the jungle. Mowgli is raised by wolves and communicates with many animals. His enemy is the tiger Shere Khan. Most of the animals follow the Law of the Jungle. *The Jungle Book* was a success, so Kipling wrote a second book the next year.

p. 31

Comprehension

1 a 2 a 3 b
4 c 5 wolves

6 c 7 b 8 e
9 a 10 d

p. 32

Reading Skills Practice: Insert Text I

A c

B

1 a 2 c 3 b

Unit 06 | *Moby-Dick*

p. 33

Pre-Reading Questions Sample Answer

1 They are trying to catch the whale.

2 The whale is looks like it is trying to get away from the men. It might be diving under the water.

3 Whaling is fishing for whales. I think whaling is okay, but we shouldn't hunt too many whales since they are an endangered species.

4 I don't think I would like that. Two years is a long time. I think one week at sea would be enough for me.

Vocabulary

1	novel	2	recognize
3	journey	4	announce
5	revenge	6	battle

p. 34

Summary

Herman Melville traveled throughout the Pacific Ocean by ship. He wrote the novels *Typee* and *Omoo* about his adventures there. Then, he wrote *Moby-Dick*. It was the great American novel. *Moby-Dick* is the story of Captain Ahab's hunt for a great white whale. The novel is about a man's quest for revenge. In the story, Moby-Dick sinks the *Pequod* and kills everyone on the ship except for Ishmael, the narrator of the story.

p. 35

Comprehension

1 a 2 b 3 a
4 c 5 novel

6 d 7 a 8 c
9 e 10 b

p. 36

Reading Skills Practice: Insert Text II

A b

B

1 a 2 c 3 a

Unit 07 | William Shakespeare

p. 37

Pre-Reading Questions Sample Answer

1 I see a picture of William Shakespeare in one picture. I see an actor in the other picture.
2 He was a playwright. He wrote a lot of plays a long time ago.
3 He was English. He lived more than 400 years ago. He also wrote many poems.
4 I think they are a little boring. I like watching movies.

Vocabulary

1 perform 2 tragedy
3 genre 4 poet
5 rhyme 6 audience

p. 38

Summary

William Shakespeare was born in 1564 and died in 1616. He came from Stratford but moved to London. Shakespeare is considered the greatest of all British writers. He wrote thirty-seven plays in three genres: history, comedy, and tragedy. *Romeo and Juliet* is one famous tragedy while *A Midsummer Night's Dream* is a well-known comedy. Shakespeare also wrote poems. He wrote 154 sonnets, which are poems with fourteen lines. Many of his sonnets are about love.

p. 39

Comprehension

1 c 2 b 3 b
4 a 5 writers

6 b 7 e 8 d
9 a 10 c

p. 40

Reading Skills Practice: Classification I

A a. history b. *Hamlet*
c. comedy d. fourteen
e. syllables f. rhyme

B

1 William Shakespeare lived during the Renaissance in England. During that time, many people began composing plays. Christopher Marlowe was one of these men. Like Shakespeare, Marlowe was born in the year 1564. However, he never achieved the great fame that Shakespeare did. One reason was that he died at the young age of twenty-nine. He was killed during a fight in a bar. Despite dying young, Marlowe wrote several plays that showed his great talent. Most of them were tragedies. For example, one of his best plays—and maybe the first one he wrote—was *Dido, Queen of Carthage*. He also composed the tragedy *Tamburlaine the Great*, which was about the emperor Timur. His most famous play was *Doctor Faustus*. In this drama, Faustus sells his soul to the Devil. In return, he receives both knowledge and power.

2 b

3 a. talent b. emperor
c. Devil d. power

Unit 08 | Edgar Allan Poe

p. 41

Pre-Reading Questions Sample Answer

1 There is a dead man on the floor. It looks like a scary picture.
2 He was an American author. He wrote a lot of scary stories.
3 They are sometimes okay. But they are often too scary for me.
4 I think *Dracula* is a horror story. So is *Frankenstein*.

Vocabulary

1 frighten
2 alcoholism
3 essay
4 struggle
5 investigator
6 mysterious

p. 42

Summary

Edgar Allan Poe wrote many different types of literature. His themes were often dark and about death. He wrote many poems like that. *The Raven* and *Annabel Lee* are two of his poems about death. Poe wrote short stories in the horror genre. His stories often have supernatural elements in them. Poe invented the detective story genre with his stories about C. Auguste Dupin. He led a difficult life and died at the age of forty.

p. 43

Comprehension

1 c
2 c
3 a
4 a
5 genres

6 c
7 e
8 d
9 a
10 b

p. 44

Reading Skills Practice: Classification II

A
a. themes
b. death
c. *Lenore*
d. supernatural
e. Invented
f. investigator

B

1

The Detective Stories of Edgar Allan Poe

a report by Nancy Davis

Edgar Allan Poe wrote all kinds of short stories. Some of his most influential short stories featured the detective C. Auguste Dupin. Dupin appeared in *The Purloined Letter*, *The Murders in the Rue Morgue*, and one other story. It was in these stories that Poe created the modern detective novel.

The Purloined Letter is a tale about a stolen letter. In this story, a letter that belongs to a lady is stolen by a minister in the government. Dupin manages to get the letter back in the story. In *The Murders in the Rue Morgue*, two women are killed in Paris. Dupin determines that it was no man, but an orangutan, that killed the women. In both stories, Dupin uses logic to solve the mysteries. I enjoyed how Dupin solved both cases.

2 b

3
a. stolen
b. minister
c. lady
d. women
e. man
f. orangutan

Chapter 3 Modern Technology

Unit 09 | Henry Ford and the Assembly Line

p. 47

Pre-Reading Questions Sample Answer

1 Some people are making a car in a factory.

2 It is like a moving belt. As objects move down the belt, people do work on them.

3 Henry Ford started an automobile company. I think he used the assembly line, too.

4 Some important businesspeople in my country's history are Lee Byungchul and Chung Juyoung. Lee was the founder of Samsung. And Chung was the founder of Hyundai.

Vocabulary

1 forever
2 nevertheless
3 install
4 found
5 afford
6 manufacture

p. 48

Summary

Henry Ford did not invent the automobile, but he greatly influenced the automotive industry. Ford founded the Ford Motor Company. It started making cars in 1903. In 1908, it produced the first Model T. The Model T quickly became so popular that the company could not make enough of them. Ford then introduced the assembly line. It was a moving belt that let workers manufacture cars more quickly than before. Overall, more than 15,000,000 Model T's were made.

p. 49

Comprehension

1 a 2 c 3 a
4 a 5 assembly line

6 b 7 c 8 a
9 e 10 d

p. 50

Reading Skills Practice: Sequencing I

A a. 1 b. 3 c. 2

B

1

William Boeing was the owner of a lumber company. In 1909, he visited Seattle on business. There, he saw his first airplane. He became interested in them. So he purchased one for himself. Boeing flew his airplane so much that he broke it. It needed new parts, but he learned that the parts would not arrive for several months. Boeing became upset and claimed that he could build a better airplane much faster. Then he founded his own airplane company in 1917. At first, Boeing made military aircraft since the United States was fighting World War I. After that his company built commercial aircraft. It quickly became a leader in the aircraft industry. In 1954, the company made its first jet. Today, the Boeing Company is the largest aerospace company in the world and makes hundreds of planes every year.

2 c
3 a. 2 b. 3 c. 1

Unit 10 | Tim Berners-Lee and the World Wide Web

p. 51

Pre-Reading Questions Sample Answer

1 I'm not really sure. I know it was made about twenty years ago.
2 I first went online when I was in kindergarten. I loved it.
3 I have my own webpage. I send email. And I like to surf some websites.
4 The Internet is fun. We can also meet new people and get lots of information. But some people use the Internet too much. And there are many bad people on the Internet as well.

Vocabulary

1 war 2 laboratory
3 link 4 complicated
5 hypertext 6 suggest

p. 52

Summary

In the 1960s, the United States government wanted a new communication system in case of war. Its researchers decided to connect computers to one another. ARPANET went online in 1969. It was the first version of the Internet. In the 1970s and 1980s, the Internet continued to develop, but it was very complicated. Then, in 1989, Tim Berners-Lee created the World Wide Web. He did that by using hypertext. He also created the world's first webpage.

p. 53

Comprehension

1 b 2 c 3 b
4 b 5 World Wide Web

6 e 7 d 8 b
9 c 10 a

p. 54

Reading Skills Practice: Sequencing II

A a. 3 b. 1 c. 2

B

1

Dear Diary,

I read an interesting article today. It was about Bill Gates. He is the one of the richest men in the world today. Here is how he became so rich. First, he became interested in computers when he was young. In fact, he started programming computers when he was only thirteen years old. Next, he went to Harvard University in 1973. At Harvard, he developed his own computer language. But he was not happy at Harvard. So, after a while, he quit going to school. Then, he focused on working at his company Microsoft. Gates started Microsoft with Paul Allen in 1975. After that, they began to develop software for personal computers. Their software became very popular in the 1980s and 1990s. So Bill Gates made a huge amount of money. He proved you can become rich through hard work.

2 b

3 a. 1 b. 3 c. 2

Unit 11 | Satellites

p. 55

Pre-Reading Questions Sample Answer

1 It is orbiting Earth.
2 They can predict the weather. They can help with communications. And they can do many other things.
3 Rockets launch them into outer space.
4 Yes, I think they are very useful. They are expensive, but they help people a lot.

Vocabulary

1	run	2	mission
3	chart	4	manmade
5	predict	6	device

p. 56

Summary

The Space Age began in 1957 when the Soviet Union launched the satellite *Sputnik*. Since then, thousands of artificial satellites have been launched. They are manmade devices that orbit other objects. Satellite can do many things. The telecommunications and cable TV industries run thanks to them. Satellites can predict the weather and run navigation systems. Militaries use them to spy on their enemies. And they are valuable for doing all kinds of research, too.

p. 57

Comprehension

1	a	2	c	3	b
4	c	5	satellite		
6	c	7	a	8	e
9	d	10	b		

p. 58

Reading Skills Practice: Summarizing I

A b

B

1

In the early years of the Space Age, many satellites were sent into space. Astronauts were also sent into space. But they only remained in orbit for a few hours or days. People desired a more permanent presence in space. So they wanted to build space stations. A space station is a spacecraft that can stay in orbit for a long time. People live and work on space stations. In the 1970s, the Americans sent *Skylab* into orbit. It orbited the Earth from 1973 to 1979. The Soviets had several space stations. They included the *Almaz* stations, the *Salyut* stations, and *Mir*. Currently, there are two space stations in orbit. They are the *International Space Station* and the Chinese space station *Tiangong-1*. Astronauts live on these space stations for extended periods of time. And they conduct many valuable experiments on them.

2 b

3 c

Unit 12 | The Industrial Revolution

p. 59

Pre-Reading Questions Sample Answer

1 There is a train on the left. And there is an old factory on the right.
2 It was a time when people started making lots of machines.
3 More people moved to cities, and fewer people

stayed on farms. And lots of kids had to work in factories during the Industrial Revolution.

4 I think it was the steam engine. It was used for many different machines.

Vocabulary

1 undergo
2 educated
3 rural
4 textile
5 factory
6 vital

p. 60

Summary

Before the 1700s, human society was based on farming. After that, the Industrial Revolution began. The Industrial Revolution started in England for many reasons. Two were that the English people were educated and the country had colonies that provided raw materials. The steam engine was the most important invention. It was used in many factories. The textile, manufacturing, and farming industries were affected by the Industrial Revolution. It caused society to change a great deal.

p. 61

Comprehension

1 c
2 a
3 b
4 a
5 farming

6 c
7 e
8 d
9 a
10 b

p. 62

Reading Skills Practice: Summarizing II

A a

B

1

August 21, 1750

Dear Mother,

All three of us have arrived in London a month ago. We have found jobs at a nearby factory. We work inside the factory making textiles all day long. We work long hours. We sometimes work up to sixteen hours a day. The factory is also not very clean, and it is dark inside, too. But we get paid, so we are happy. My brothers and I live in a small place near our factory. Lots of other workers from the factory live nearby. We are sorry that we did not stay on the farm with you and Father. But we felt that we had to get away from the countryside. Because of the new machines, fewer people are needed on farms these days. And factories in London are always hiring new workers.

Your son,
Ian

2 c

3 b

Chapter 4 Economics

Unit 13 | The Silk Road

p. 65

Pre-Reading Questions Sample Answer

1 They are crossing a desert on camels.
2 It was in Asia. It went from China to the Middle East.
3 I guess they trade silk. And they probably traded spices and gold, too.
4 It was probably difficult. And I think it was also dangerous.

Vocabulary

1 desired
2 route
3 typically
4 bandit
5 major
6 destination

p. 66

Summary

Most people traded with individuals close to them. But there was some long-distance trade in the past. Rome and China traded on the Silk Road. The Silk Road was not one road. It was numerous routes that started in China and went across Asia and then to Rome. The Silk Road was dangerous, but many merchants traded on it. They traded lots of goods, including silk. A large number of merchants became wealthy from trading on the Silk Road.

p. 67

Comprehension

1 c 2 a 3 b
4 c 5 Roman

6 d 7 e 8 b
9 a 10 c

p. 68

Reading Skills Practice: Cause and Effect I

A a. iii b. i c. ii

B

1 In the 1600s and 1700s, England had many colonies in North America. The people in the colonies were eager to trade. So a trading system developed. It was called Triangle Trade. It involved England, Africa, and the American colonies. Ships left England and went to Africa. They carried items like beads, weapons, and cloth. They traded them for African slaves. The slaves were loaded onto other ships. Those ships sailed to America. The American colonists needed many people to work on their plantations. So they bought the slaves that arrived on the ships. That was the second part of Triangle Trade. The third part involved shipping raw materials to England. Because England had many factories, it needed lots of raw materials to make finished products. So the colonists shipped sugar, tobacco, cotton, wood, and other goods to England.

2 a

3 a. so b. Because c. Since

Unit 14 | Bartering

p. 69

Pre-Reading Questions Sample Answer

1 Someone is trading some water for some corn.
2 People barter because they want to trade items with each other.
3 Yes, I have. I traded a baseball for some marbles once.
4 I think bartering is fun.

Vocabulary

1 service 2 lack
3 poor 4 civilization
5 agree 6 worthless

p. 70

Summary

In the past, there was no money, so people bartered for the goods and services they needed. Bartering involves trading certain items for others. Even after money was invented, people continued to barter. Some of these people lacked money, but they had goods and services to trade. Other people did not have a use for money. And some people lived in countries with poor economies. Their money was worthless, so they had to barter.

p. 71

Comprehension

1 b 2 b 3 a
4 c 5 money

6 d 7 b 8 e
9 c 10 a

p. 72

Reading Skills Practice: Cause and Effect II

A a. i b. iii c. ii

B

1 Dear Diary,

Today at school, we learned about money. Most countries use paper bills and coins as money nowadays. But it was different in the past. Societies used different objects as money. Many cultures valued metals like gold and silver. So they made gold and silver coins and used them as money. But some cultures did not have any gold or silver. So they found other items and used them as money. In Roman times, the army sometimes paid soldiers with salt. It was actually much more valuable than money, so the soldiers did not mind being paid that way. In the Netherlands a few centuries ago, people used tulip bulbs as money. And some ancient tribes used giant rocks or shells as money. Since the rocks and shells were rare, the tribes thought that they were worth a lot.

2 c

3 a. Because b. Therefore c. so

Unit 15 | Franchises

p. 73

Pre-Reading Questions Sample Answer

1 It is a company that has many branches in different places.

2 KFC, McDonald's, and Burger King are franchises. So are the Hilton Hotel and the Holiday Inn.

3 I think they are okay. I like that I can eat KFC chicken in many places.

4 Franchises often provide goods or services for cheap prices. They are common in many places. I'm not really sure about their disadvantages.

Vocabulary

1	supply	2	right
3	entire	4	train
5	highly	6	spread

p. 74

Summary

Many cities and towns around the world have franchises. A franchise is the right for someone to sell a good or service belonging to another company. A lot of fast-food restaurants are franchises. But other businesses have franchises, too. Franchises have several advantages. They are good for first-time business owners. The companies provide support in many ways. Franchises started in the 1800s and have spread around the world today. A lot of them are highly successful companies.

p. 75

Comprehension

1	a	2	b	3	b
4	c	5	business		
6	c	7	d	8	a
9	e	10	b		

p. 76

Reading Skills Practice: Identifying Cohesive Devices I

A a. In addition b. However c. when

B

1 In 1940, two brothers, Richard and Maurice McDonald, opened a restaurant in San Bernardino, California. They called it McDonald's. They wanted to become rich. So they worked very hard. They also developed a new system for preparing food. It was based on the assembly line. As a result they could prepare food very quickly. Then, in 1954, Ray Kroc began to work with the McDonald brothers. He realized the potential of the restaurant. So he wanted to expand it around the world. But the brothers did not want to expand quickly. So Kroc purchased the rights to the restaurant from the McDonald brothers. Kroc made them rich, but he became the owner. Then he opened franchises in the United States. In addition McDonald's franchises started opening in other countries. Today, there are more than 34,000 McDonald's franchises in 119 countries.

2 c

3 a. also b. so c. but

Unit 16 | Changes in the U.S. Dollar

p. 77

Pre-Reading Questions Sample Answer

1 I can see lots of American money in the picture on the left. On the right, I can see money from many different countries. I'm not sure which countries though.

2 Yes, I have. My uncle went to the U.S., and he gave me a dollar when he came back.
3 My country is Korea. We use won in Korea.
4 Japan uses the yen. Thailand uses the baht. Many countries in Europe use the euro.

Vocabulary

1	recognized	2	coming
3	bill	4	counterfeit
5	value	6	prepare

p. 78

Summary

The U.S. dollar is used around the world, and many people recognize it. But it has not always looked like it does today. The first dollars were printed by the Massachusetts Bay Colony in 1690. The American colonists also printed Continental Currency in 1775. But the first real American dollars were printed in 1785. Since then, the design of the dollar has changed a lot. For instance, the images on the ten-dollar bill have changed frequently.

p. 79

Comprehension

1	c	2	a	3	c
4	a	5	changed		
6	c	7	a	8	e
9	d	10	b		

p. 80

Reading Skills Practice: Identifying Cohesive Devices II

A b

B

1

Dear Sally,

I just arrived in the United States. I am looking forward to studying here. The country is nice, but the money can be very confusing. There are several types of bills and coins. The bills are easy to use. However, the coins are confusing because they all have names. And many Americans use the names of the coins instead of their values. For instance, a one-cent coin is called a penny. A five-cent coin is a nickel. A ten-cent coin is a dime. And a twenty-five-cent coin is a quarter. They even have fifty-cent coins and dollar coins. But those coins lack special names. I need to remember the names of the coins to make my time here more comfortable. I forgot them the last time I went shopping. So I was a little embarrassed.

Your friend,
Julie

2 a
3 b

Chapter 5 Ancient Societies

Unit 17 | Ancient Egypt

p. 83

Pre-Reading Questions Sample Answer

1 I can see some ruins next to a river. I guess it is the Nile River.
2 It was very important. It gave people in Egypt water.
3 I know Ramses was a pharaoh. I think Cleopatra was one, too.
4 The ancient Egyptians made the pyramids. They also made the Sphinx. They had a kingdom for a long time.

Vocabulary

1	flow	2	farm
3	pharaoh	4	neighboring
5	arise	6	source

p. 84

Summary

The Nile River flows through Egypt on its way to the Mediterranean Sea. Thanks to the Nile, an ancient civilization arose in Egypt thousands of years ago. The pharaohs ruled Egypt for nearly 3,000 years. They were like gods to the Egyptians. Under the pharaohs, Egypt became the most powerful empire in Africa and the Middle East. The Egyptians constructed numerous pyramids and monuments. Today, people can still see many of them.

p. 85

Comprehension

1 b 2 b 3 a
4 c 5 pyramids

6 c 7 a 8 d
9 b 10 e

p. 86

Reading Skills Practice: Outlining I

A a. Nile River b. floods
c. pharaohs d. empire
e. Constructed

B
1 a. Tigris b. cities
c. Sumerians d. writing
e. laws
2 b

Unit 18 | The Chinese Qin Dynasty

p. 87

Pre-Reading Questions Sample Answer

1 I can see lots of statues of people in the picture.
2 I think they were found in China.
3 I don't know exactly, but I think it was a long time ago.
4 There used to be a big empire in ancient China. The Chinese built the Great Wall then.

Vocabulary

1 protect 2 dynasty
3 chariot 4 measure
5 kingdom 6 declare

p. 88

Summary

In 221 B.C., Qin Shi Huangdi united China and founded the Qin Dynasty. The dynasty did not last long, but it was very important to China. China became larger than ever. There were many road construction projects, and work was done on the Great Wall of China. Qin Shi Huangdi also standardized writing, laws, weights, measures, and currency. When the emperor died, he was buried near Xian with an army of terracotta warriors. His tomb was discovered in 1974.

p. 89

Comprehension

1 c 2 a 3 b
4 c 5 warriors

6 d 7 a 8 e
9 b 10 c

p. 90

Reading Skills Practice: Outlining II

A a. unified b. dynasty
c. writing d. tomb
e. terracotta f. statues

B
1 a. 2,500 b. invaders
c. 7,000 d. engineering
e. hundreds
2 c

Unit 19 | Harappan Civilization

p. 91

Pre-Reading Questions Sample Answer

1 It looks like a field with some ruins in it.
2 I'm not really sure. I think it was in Asia.
3 It was probably thousands of years old.
4 I know people in *Gojoseon* used bronze tools like swords, daggers, and spears. They also had *goindol*, a kind of tomb.

Vocabulary

1 bronze 2 relic
3 severe 4 hieroglyphics
5 collapse 6 vanish

p. 92

Summary

A lot of ancient civilizations vanished without a trace. Others left ruins and relics that archaeologists study. The Harappan Civilization is mysterious. It existed in the Indus River Valley from around 3300 B.C. to 2000 B.C. The Harappan people built cities with a grid system. They made bronze tools and wrote with hieroglyphics. But Harappan society suddenly collapsed around 2000 B.C. Archaeologists are not sure why. There may have been a severe drought. Or invaders may have killed them.

p. 93

Comprehension

1 a	2 c	3 a
4 b	5 ruins	
6 c	7 e	8 a
9 d	10 b	

p. 94

Reading Skills Practice: Simplifying I

A c

B

1

The Harappan people had their own religion. They worshipped many gods. After the Harappan Civilization fell, a new group of people settled in India. They had their own gods. But these new people also took some of the Harappan gods and made them their own. Centuries later, Hinduism developed. The *Rig Veda* is the earliest known writing about Hinduism. It was probably created around 1000 B.C. But it was not written down until about 300 B.C. Before then, people either sang or spoke it. Hinduism was a polytheistic religion. So it had a large number of gods. Vishnu and Shiva were two of the most important Hindu gods, but there were many others. They included Indra, Ganesha, Kali, and Krishna. Over the years, Hinduism became the dominant religion in India. Today, millions of people around the world practice it.

2 b

3 a

Unit 20 | The Aztec Empire

p. 95

Pre-Reading Questions Sample Answer

1 Some of them are wearing armor. They look like they are going to fight. One man looks like he is wearing a bird costume.

2 It was in Mexico.

3 The Aztecs lived a long time ago. They liked to fight. The Spanish killed most of them though.

4 The Incas and Mayas lived in the Americas. The Eskimos live in America, too.

Vocabulary

1 warlike	2 nomadic
3 ally	4 eager
5 establish	6 battle

p. 96

Summary

The Aztecs built a city called Tenochtitlan and founded the Aztec Empire. Tenochtitlan was the Aztecs' power base. In the 1400s and 1500s, they won many wars and expanded the size of their empire. The neighboring tribes feared the Aztecs. The reason was that the Aztecs took prisoners and then killed them during religious ceremonies. When the Spanish arrived in 1519, the nearby tribes joined them to fight the Aztecs. In 1521, the Spanish defeated the Aztec Empire.

p. 97

Comprehension

1 c	2 a	3 c
4 b	5 Spanish	
6 e	7 d	8 a
9 b	10 c	

p. 98

Reading Skills Practice: Simplifying II

A b

B

1

Dear Kelly,

I am still on vacation in Mexico, and I am visiting a lot of ancient sites. They are so fascinating. The other day, I visited a place called Chichen Itza. It used to be a large city. But today there are only ruins. It was a city that was built by the Mayans. The Mayan Empire existed in Central America many centuries ago. The Mayans were powerful from around the years 600 to 1200. Can you imagine that? They had a great civilization in the rainforests of Central America for at least 600 years. That is incredible. Then, something happened to the Mayans. No one is exactly sure what happened, but Mayan society suddenly became weak, so the Mayan Empire collapsed. I wonder what took place. It must have been a bad event.

Your friend,
Alice

2 c

3 c

Word List

Word List

Chapter 1 Weather

Unit 01

1 **condition** *(n)* a requirement; a situation
The man is in bad ***condition*** because of his illness.

2 **deadly** *(adj)* fatal; causing death
The bites of many snakes can be ***deadly*** to people.

3 **enormous** *(adj)* very large; great; huge
You spend an ***enormous*** amount of time watching television.

4 **flooding** *(n)* a situation in a which a body of water rises above its normal level
Expect ***flooding*** to happen until it stops raining.

5 **heavily** *(adv)* greatly; very much
Dan gambled ***heavily***, so he lost most of his money.

6 **measure** *(v)* to determine; to calculate
We need to ***measure*** the distance between these two points.

7 **necessary** *(adj)* required; needed
It is not ***necessary*** for you to go to the train station with me.

8 **perish** *(v)* to die
Thousands of people ***perished*** because of the hurricane.

9 **refer** *(v)* to talk about something; to give a name to
We ***refer*** to our homeroom teacher as Mr. Parker.

10 **region** *(n)* an area; a place
Some ***regions*** of the country get a large amount of rain.

Unit 02

1 **avoid** *(v)* to keep away from; not to see or meet
Sally tries to ***avoid*** Mark since she does not like him.

2 **basement** *(n)* the lowest level of a building and which is often underground
Many people use the ***basements*** in their homes for storage.

3 **crash** *(v)* to run into; to hit
He lost control of his bicycle and ***crashed*** into a tree.

4 **gently** *(adv)* softly
Gently comb your dog's fur, or you could hurt it.

5 **hide** *(v)* to find a place of safety and to keep from being seen
The children are going to ***hide*** when their teacher comes into the room.

6 **remain** *(v)* to stay in a certain place
Please ***remain*** here while I run into the store for a moment.

7 **roof** *(n)* the top outer part of a building
There is a bird's nest on the ***roof*** of that building.

8 **siren** *(n)* an alarm that makes a very loud noise
The ***siren*** only goes off when there is a tornado or severe storm.

9 **underneath** *(prep)* beneath; below
If you look ***underneath*** the desk, you will find the bag.

10 **upstairs** *(adv)* on or to an upper level of a building
I sleep ***upstairs***, but my brother sleeps downstairs.

Unit 03

1 **atmosphere** *(n)* the air
The Earth's ***atmosphere*** extends far above the planet's surface.

2 **continual** *(adj)* happening again and again; constant; at all times
Your ***continual*** complaints are starting to bother me.

3 **cycle** *(n)* a series; a complete set of events that is repeated
This is a ***cycle*** that has been going on for years.

4 **encounter** *(v)* to meet; to run into
They ***encountered*** the movie star while they were walking on the street.

5 **pleasant** *(adj)* nice
The weather today is so ***pleasant*** that many people are spending time outside.

6 **precipitation** *(n)* water in any form that falls from the sky
There is going to be a lot of ***precipitation*** this week.

7 **predict** *(v)* to guess; to make a guess about the future
What do you ***predict*** is going to happen in the future?

8 **reuse** *(v)* to use again
You should always try to ***reuse*** certain products.

9 **sleet** *(n)* frozen rain
When ***sleet*** is falling, driving on the roads can be dangerous.

10 **tiny** *(adj)* very small
I love your paper, but you need to make a couple of ***tiny*** changes.

Unit 04

1 **blizzard** *(n)* a storm in which snow falls so much that one can only see white
You should stay indoors anytime there is a ***blizzard***.

2 **damage** *(v)* to harm; to hurt; to injure
You ***damaged*** the window when you hit it with a baseball.

3 **definitely** *(adv)* for sure; positively
I will ***definitely*** have enough time to attend your birthday party.

4 **experience** *(n)* an event
Visiting Africa was such a wonderful ***experience***.

5 **release** *(v)* to let go
John always ***releases*** any fish he catches back into the water.

6 **scared** *(adj)* frightened; afraid
Cathy said that she was not ***scared*** of the big dog.

7 **true** *(adj)* factual; not false
It is ***true*** that eating fast food can be unhealthy.

8 **unusual** *(adj)* not normal; uncommon
The weather is cold today, which is ***unusual*** for this time of year.

9 **wrong** *(adj)* incorrect; not right
You wrote down the ***wrong*** answer to this question.

10 **yell** *(v)* to speak very loudly; to shout
Please do not ***yell*** since I have a headache.

Chapter 2 **Literature**

Unit 05

1 **abroad** *(adv)* in a foreign country
They are going to travel ***abroad*** this winter vacation.

2 **adventure** *(n)* a journey; a quest; an exciting activity
Kevin had an exciting ***adventure*** rafting down the Amazon River.

3 **communicate** *(v)* to speak with
It is often fun to ***communicate*** in a foreign language.

4 **follow** *(v)* to obey; to listen to
Be sure to ***follow*** my advice very closely, or you will have problems.

5 **greatly** *(adv)* very much
Everyone was ***greatly*** impressed by Sue's knowledge.

6 **lair** *(n)* the underground home of an animal
It is dangerous to enter the ***lairs*** of some wild animals, such as bears.

7 **particularly** *(adv)* quite; very
I am ***particularly*** interested in learning more about the subject.

8 **protect** *(v)* to guard; to keep safe
The cat is ***protecting*** its kittens from the dog.

9 **raise** *(v)* to take care of someone while he or she is a child
Emily's parents ***raised*** her to be a nice young woman.

10 **success** *(n)* a victory; an achievement
Steve's business trip was a ***success*** since the company agreed to his offer.

Unit 06

1 **actually** *(adv)* really
Frank ***actually*** majored in biology even though he is a music teacher.

2 **crew** *(n)* a group of people who work on a ship, boat, or train
Tom is one of the ***crew*** on the ship.

3 **destination** *(n)* the place that a person is going to
Be sure to write your ***destination*** on the immigration form.

4 **explore** *(v)* to investigate; to travel around
The adventurers are going to ***explore*** the jungle for a week.

5 **hunt** *(n)* a chase after an animal
The ***hunt*** was successful as they captured several animals.

6 **incredible** *(adj)* amazing
We watched the most ***incredible*** magician perform on TV.

7 **instance** *(n)* an event; an example
The fire was an ***instance*** of an event that was caused on purpose.

8 **novel** *(n)* a book of fiction
Her new ***novel*** will be published sometime next year.

9 **ram** *(v)* to run into, often on purpose
In ancient times, ships used to try to ***ram*** others when they were fighting.

10 **reach** *(v)* to arrive; to get to the place one is going
We should ***reach*** our destination in about ten minutes.

Unit 07

1 **achieve** *(v)* to do; to be successful at something
You can ***achieve*** anything if you try hard enough.

2 **actor** *(n)* a male performer
Charlie Chaplin was one of the most famous ***actors*** of his time.

3 **comedy** *(n)* a type of work that makes people laugh; a work of humor
I prefer ***comedies*** to tragedies when watching plays.

4 **compose** *(v)* to create a work of writing, art, or music
Some people can ***compose*** great works in a short period of time.

5 **enjoy** *(v)* to like very much
Sara ***enjoys*** spending time with her friends on the weekend.

6 **excellent** *(adj)* outstanding; very good; wonderful
Please tell the chef that dinner was ***excellent***.

7 **knowledge** *(n)* information; data; facts
The library is a great place to acquire more ***knowledge***.

8 **lifetime** *(n)* the time from one's birth to death
Mr. Jones earned millions of dollars during his ***lifetime***.

9 **poem** *(n)* a type of writing in verse
Writing a ***poem*** is much harder than writing a story.

10 **talent** *(n)* skill; ability
It requires ***talent*** and hard work to become a great actor.

Unit 08

1 **battle** *(v)* to fight
The two armies ***battled*** each other for several hours.

2 **contain** *(v)* to have; to possess
According to the label, this food ***contains*** many vitamins and minerals.

3 **detective** *(n)* a person who investigates mysteries such as crimes
Sherlock Holmes is a ***detective*** in stories written by Arthur Conan Doyle.

4 **determine** *(v)* to figure out; to solve a problem
Let's try to ***determine*** what the problem is.

5 **especially** *(adv)* particularly; mainly
Janet was ***especially*** pleased with the present her parents gave her.

6 **feature** *(v)* to be about; to have
The documentary ***features*** an interview with Dr. Taylor.

7 **focus** *(v)* to emphasize; to stress
You had better ***focus*** on doing well on your final exams.

8 **masque** *(n)* a party in which the people there wear masks; a masquerade ball
Everyone wore fancy costumes when they attended the ***masque***.

9 **minister** *(n)* a high-ranking government worker
The education ***minister*** resigned because of a scandal.

10 **scary** *(adj)* frightening
Stories about ghosts and monsters are ***scary*** to many people.

Chapter 3 Modern Technology

Unit 09

1 **claim** *(v)* to declare; to state; to announce
Sam ***claims*** that he knows how to solve that problem.

2 **goods** *(n)* products
The workers loaded many ***goods*** onto the truck.

3 **introduce** *(v)* to start; to begin
The teacher ***introduced*** some scientific concepts to the students.

4 **leader** *(n)* the person who is in charge; a boss
Please tell your ***leader*** that I want to speak with him.

5 **lumber** *(n)* wood that is used for making things
They are going to use the ***lumber*** to build some furniture.

6 **military** *(n)* the armed forces; the army
The ***military*** in that country is growing bigger every year.

7 **part** *(n)* a piece; a division
This machine will not work since it is missing a few ***parts***.

8 **produce** *(v)* to make; to manufacture
Do you know what that factory ***produces***?

9 **single** *(adj)* one
There is a ***single*** bottle of water sitting on the shelf.

10 **supply** *(n)* the amount of something; how much of something there is
The company's ***supply*** of that product is getting lower because it is selling well.

Unit 10

1 **add** *(v)* to join; to attach
After you ***add*** this part to the machine, it will work much better.

2 **billion** *(n)* 1,000,000,000; a thousand million
Some people who started their own companies become worth ***billions*** of dollars.

3 **develop** *(v)* to create; to make
Try to ***develop*** your own ideas and then figure out how to make money from them.

4 **early** *(adj)* first; near the beginning
Early humans could only use very simple tools.

5 **huge** *(adj)* very large; enormous
You made a ***huge*** mistake, so we have to start over.

6 **program** *(v)* to give instructions to a computer
How long will it take to ***program*** the computer?

7 **prove** *(v)* to show that something is true
The police ***proved*** that the man had stolen the diamonds.

8 **quit** *(v)* to stop; to halt
They always ***quit*** working at six thirty every day.

9 **researcher** *(n)* a person who studies something in depth; a person who does research
A ***researcher*** in that laboratory discovered a new element.

10 **software** *(n)* a computer program
My brother designs ***software*** for a computer game company.

Unit 11

1 **astronaut** *(n)* a person who goes into space and works there

The ***astronaut*** spent more than six months in the space station.

2 **circle** *(v)* to go around something; to make a circle around something

The planes are ***circling*** the airport as they wait to land.

3 **desire** *(v)* to want

Tell me what you ***desire***, and I will try to get it for you.

4 **extended** *(adj)* long; lengthy

The cousins talked for an ***extended*** period of time.

5 **freeze** *(v)* to change from a liquid or a gas to a solid

Water begins to ***freeze*** at zero degrees Celsius.

6 **melt** *(v)* to change from a solid or a gas to a liquid

You must heat iron to a high temperature to get it to ***melt***.

7 **object** *(n)* a thing

I cannot identify the ***object*** he has in his hand.

8 **observe** *(v)* to see; to look at; to notice

They will ***observe*** the animals in their habitat for at least a week.

9 **permanent** *(adj)* forever; for all time

If you use ***permanent*** ink, you will not be able to erase your writing.

10 **purpose** *(n)* a reason

Joey will explain the ***purpose*** of the meeting in a few minutes.

Unit 12

1 **affect** *(v)* to influence; to have an effect on

Caffeine ***affects*** many people by making them more alert.

2 **countryside** *(n)* an area outside a city or town; a rural area

My family is going to spend the summer months in the ***countryside***.

3 **farm** *(n)* a place where people grow crops and raise animals

My father grew up on a ***farm*** that had many cows and pigs.

4 **hire** *(v)* to give a job to; to employ

The company plans to ***hire*** several new employees this year.

5 **industry** *(n)* a type of business; manufacturing

The automobile ***industry*** is very powerful in this country.

6 **overall** *(adv)* covering everything

Overall, everyone is pleased with your performance.

7 **place** *(n)* a home; a house

Janet has a nice ***place*** in the downtown area.

8 **power** *(n)* energy

The company uses a lot of ***power*** to operate all of its machines.

9 **revolution** *(n)* a rebellion; a time when there is great change in society

There may be a ***revolution*** if the government continues spying on its own people.

10 **society** *(n)* civilization; a group of people that live together

There is a strong ***society*** whose people obey the laws.

Chapter 4 Economics

Unit 13

1 **cross** *(v)* to go across; to go over
You can ***cross*** the river at a bridge just past the hill.

2 **eager** *(adj)* willing; excited about
Tim is ***eager*** to get started on the new project.

3 **individual** *(n)* a person
Alice is an ***individual*** who likes to meet all kinds of people.

4 **load** *(v)* to put on board a ship, truck, or other vehicle
The men are ***loading*** the boxes onto the truck.

5 **numerous** *(adj)* many
There are ***numerous*** problems with the company's software.

6 **offer** *(v)* to propose; to say that one will do something
We want to know what you plan to ***offer*** for our services.

7 **plantation** *(n)* a very large farm
Many ***plantations*** used to grow cotton and tobacco.

8 **ship** *(v)* to transport goods, often over the water
The company ***ships*** all of its products by airplane.

9 **slave** *(n)* a person who is owned by another
There are still ***slaves*** in parts of Africa and the Middle East today.

10 **triangle** *(n)* a closed object that has three sides
Use a ruler to draw a ***triangle*** with three equal sides.

Unit 14

1 **barter** *(v)* to trade one thing for another
I plan to ***barter*** for the things I need since I have no money.

2 **bill** *(n)* paper money
Most men keep ***bills*** in their wallets.

3 **convenient** *(adj)* fitting; suitable
It would be ***convenient*** for me if you arrive a little early.

4 **fix** *(v)* to repair; to make better
Do you know how to ***fix*** a bicycle?

5 **nowadays** *(adv)* at the present; currently
Nowadays, many people are purchasing e-books.

6 **pay** *(v)* to give money to a person for work done or to purchase something
You should ***pay*** the cashier for the items you buy.

7 **rare** *(adj)* uncommon; unusual
That looks like a ***rare*** flower that you have found.

8 **shell** *(n)* the hard outer covering of animals such as clams and oysters
The ***shells*** of many oysters are difficult for people to open.

9 **tribe** *(n)* a group of people who are similar to one another
There are some primitive ***tribes*** that still live in the Amazon Rainforest.

10 **worth** *(adj)* having a value of
That necklace appears to be ***worth*** a lot of money.

Unit 15

1 **assistance** *(n)* help

I can give you some ***assistance*** if you need any.

2 **employee** *(n)* a worker

There are several ***employees*** working in the office now.

3 **expand** *(v)* to make larger

Paul is making plans to ***expand*** his company into some foreign countries.

4 **operate** *(v)* to run; to use

Please show us how to ***operate*** this machine.

5 **owner** *(n)* a person who possesses something

Talk to the ***owner*** if you have any complaints.

6 **potential** *(adj)* possible; probable

Sam is a ***potential*** honors student if he would just study more.

7 **prepare** *(v)* to get ready

You need to ***prepare*** for the dinner party tonight.

8 **purchase** *(v)* to buy

When we go to the store, you can ***purchase*** anything you want.

9 **realize** *(v)* to notice; to understand

Do they ***realize*** how important this meeting is?

10 **similar** *(adj)* like; alike

They do not know each other, but they use many ***similar*** expressions.

Unit 16

1 **colony** *(n)* an area of land that belongs to another country

Many European countries had ***colonies*** in Asia, Africa, and the Americas.

2 **confusing** *(adj)* hard to understand

This report is ***confusing***, so can you explain it to me?

3 **continental** *(adj)* relating to a continent

Continental drift explains how the landmasses on the Earth move around.

4 **currency** *(n)* money

Japanese ***currency*** is called yen while the money in Korea is called won.

5 **decade** *(n)* a period of ten years

Sarah has been alive for almost three ***decades***.

6 **embarrassed** *(adj)* self-conscious; feeling humiliated about something

When I could not remember the words to my speech, I was very ***embarrassed***.

7 **forget** *(v)* not to remember

Robert never ***forgets*** anything that he reads.

8 **print** *(v)* to make money

The government plans to ***print*** more money next year.

9 **quarter** *(n)* an American coin worth twenty-five cents

I need to put one more ***quarter*** in the vending machine to get a drink.

10 **value** *(n)* worth

The ***value*** of a good education cannot be measured.

Chapter 5 Ancient Societies

Unit 17

1 **advance** *(n)* an improvement; a development
The scientists made several ***advances*** in the past year.

2 **builder** *(v)* a person who builds or makes things
The Romans were some of the greatest ***builders*** in ancient times.

3 **conquer** *(v)* to defeat in battle
Alexander's armies ***conquered*** many lands in Asia.

4 **construct** *(v)* to make; to build
It will take about three years to ***construct*** the building.

5 **form** *(v)* to create; to establish
Some of the students want to ***form*** a swimming club.

6 **journey** *(n)* a trip
We will go on a ***journey*** through many countries in South America.

7 **kingdom** *(n)* the land that is ruled by a king
The king travels through his ***kingdom*** each year to speak with the people.

8 **progress** *(v)* to advance; to develop
You must ***progress*** to the next level by next month.

9 **sea** *(n)* a large body of salt water
The Caribbean ***Sea*** is located between North and South America.

10 **transport** *(v)* to move from one place to another
The company needs several trucks to ***transport*** the goods it is selling.

Unit 18

1 **act** *(n)* a feat; a deed; an action
Rick committed an ***act*** of heroism by saving the drowning swimmer.

2 **army** *(n)* a large group of soldiers
Many young men are interested in joining the ***army***.

3 **bury** *(v)* to put under the ground and to cover with dirt
Dogs like to ***bury*** bones and other objects in the ground.

4 **discovery** *(n)* something that a person finds
The accidental ***discovery*** of penicillin changed the medical world.

5 **emperor** *(n)* a person who rules an empire; a king
The ***emperor*** stepped down and let his son take control.

6 **foreign** *(adj)* from another country
Henry's sister has lived in a ***foreign*** country for five years.

7 **invader** *(n)* a person who attacks land belonging to another
A group of ***invaders*** attacked the town for several days.

8 **protect** *(v)* to keep someone or something safe
The guards will try to ***protect*** the people to keep them safe.

9 **site** *(n)* a place; a location
Historians believe this is the ***site*** of an ancient battle.

10 **unify** *(v)* to bring together; to unite
The leaders agreed to ***unify*** their countries soon.

Unit 19

1 **dominant** *(adj)* more powerful; stronger; leading
The ***dominant*** animal always leads the pack.

2 **mystery** *(n)* something that is unknown
It is a ***mystery*** how the thieves stole the diamonds.

3 **palace** *(n)* the home of a king or emperor
The king's ***palace*** is the largest building in the city.

4 **polytheistic** *(adj)* having many gods
There are many ***polytheistic*** religions in cultures around the world.

5 **pottery** *(n)* ceramics that are plates, pots, bowls, or other items used for eating
The archaeologists found some pieces of ***pottery*** in the old building.

6 **ruins** *(n)* the remains of a destroyed building
There are many ***ruins*** of ancient buildings in Rome and Athens.

7 **temple** *(n)* a building in which people practice their religion
The priests are holding a ceremony in the ***temple***.

8 **tool** *(n)* an object that is used to do work
You can buy many ***tools*** at the hardware store.

9 **urban** *(adj)* relating to the city
Living in an ***urban*** environment is different from living in the country.

10 **worship** *(v)* to pray to one's god
Many people ***worship*** in church every Sunday.

Unit 20

1 **capture** *(v)* to catch; to seize
The zookeepers will try to ***capture*** the escaped animals.

2 **collapse** *(v)* to fall apart; to end
When the bridge ***collapsed***, there were several cars driving across it.

3 **event** *(n)* a happening; an occasion
This was the most exciting ***event*** in the city's history.

4 **fascinating** *(adj)* interesting
We had a ***fascinating*** vacation when we went on a safari to Africa.

5 **master** *(n)* a leader; a boss
In the past, slaves always had to obey their ***master***.

6 **neighboring** *(adj)* nearby; next to
The citizens of the city are upset with the actions of the ***neighboring*** town.

7 **perform** *(v)* to do; to act
He is going to ***perform*** an impressive act of bravery.

8 **prisoner** *(n)* a person who has been captured by another
There are more than 500 ***prisoners*** in the jail.

9 **rainforest** *(n)* a forest with many trees and that gets a large amount of rain
A great number of plant and animal species live in the ***rainforest***.

10 **weak** *(adj)* having no power; not strong
Brenda feels ***weak*** because she has been sick for more than a month.

memo

Mastering Reading Skills

Michael A. Putlack

2

Workbook

DARAKWON

Mastering Reading Skills 2

Workbook

DARAKWON

C h a p t e r

1

Weather

UNIT 01 Hurricanes

A Read the passage on page 12 again. Then, write the answers to the questions.

1 Where do hurricanes form?

____

2 How warm must the water be for a hurricane to form?

____

3 How fast are the wind speeds of some hurricanes?

____

4 How long can some hurricanes last?

____

5 Why do some hurricanes cause flooding?

____

B Use the words in the box to complete the sentences. You may need to change the forms of the words.

rotate	loss of life	tropical storm	be uprooted	storm surge

1 Thankfully, there was no ______________ when the hurricane hit the city.

2 Several trees ______________ because the wind blew hard all night long.

3 Earth takes twenty-four hours to ______________ once.

4 The ______________ brought a huge wave of water onto land.

5 There is a ______________ dropping a lot of rain near Africa right now.

C Read the passage on page 14 again. Then, fill in the blanks with the correct words.

1 A tropical storm in ________________ is called a typhoon.

2 A ________________ is a tropical storm in the Indian Ocean.

3 Hurricanes and typhoons are the ________________ type of storm.

4 The deadliest storm in history happened in ________________.

5 In 2008, a cyclone in ________________ killed at least 100,000 people.

D Read the passage. Then, underline the details about the Great Galveston Hurricane and circle the details about the damage the Great Galveston Hurricane did.

The city of Galveston, Texas, is on the coast of the Gulf of Mexico. On September 8, 1900, it was hit by a Category 4 hurricane. A Category 5 hurricane is the most powerful of all storms. But the Great Galveston Hurricane was still very strong. It had winds that blew more than 200 kilometers per hour. It also dropped a great amount of rain. The storm surge from the hurricane was more than four meters high. Before the storm, Galveston was the largest city in Texas. But, after the hurricane, the city was almost entirely destroyed. Around 8,000 people in Galveston were killed. That made it the deadliest hurricane in American history. In addition, hundreds of homes and other buildings were destroyed. Many ships were sunk. The hurricane caused millions of dollars of damage, too.

UNIT 02 Tornadoes

A Read the passage on page 16 again. Then, write the answers to the questions.

1 Where did Dorothy and Toto hide from a tornado in *The Wizard of OZ*?

____

2 When do most tornadoes form?

____

3 How fast can the winds of some tornadoes move?

____

4 Which country gets a lot of tornadoes?

____

5 What is Tornado Alley?

____

B Use the words in the box to complete the sentences. You may need to change the forms of the words.

resident	storm cloud	spinning air	thunderstorm	utterly

1 We were ________________ shocked when Mr. Thompson got very angry.

2 Because of the ________________ in the sky, it may start raining soon.

3 There was a great deal of lightning during last night's ________________.

4 How many ________________ of this town are there?

5 A tornado contains ________________ that moves very quickly.

C Read the passage on page 18 again. Then, answer T (true) or F (false).

1 _______ The writer heard sirens while watching TV.

2 _______ The writer's parents said that a tornado was coming.

3 _______ The writer's family hid in the garage.

4 _______ A tree crashed through the roof of the writer's house.

5 _______ No houses on the writer's street were destroyed.

D Read the passage. Then, underline the details about the tornado drill and circle the details about the reason for the tornado drill.

Dear Diary,

Today, something unique happened at school today: We had a tornado drill. It was similar to a fire drill, but we acted differently for the tornado drill. First, a bell at the school ran three times. That was the signal for the drill to begin. The students all lined up by the door. Then, we all went into the hallway. We all sat down on the floor and put our jackets over our heads. After that, we put our heads between our knees. All of the students made sure to stay away from glass windows and doors. When the drill ended, we went back to our classrooms. We had the drill because tornado season is coming. We ought to be prepared. Last spring, there were three tornadoes near our town. I hope that no tornadoes form here this year.

UNIT

03 The Water Cycle

A Read the passage on page 20 again. Then, write the answers to the questions.

1 What are the four stages of the water cycle?

____

2 What happens during the evaporation stage?

____

3 What are clouds made of?

____

4 What happens when a cloud becomes too heavy?

____

5 What are some forms of precipitation?

____

B Use the words in the box to complete the sentences. You may need to change the forms of the words.

process	hail	droplet	groundwater	water vapor

1 You can see ______________ when water is boiling on a stove.

2 Please describe the ______________ that you will use in the experiment.

3 Many people dig wells to get access to ______________ beneath the surface.

4 Some of the ______________ that fell in the morning damaged cars.

5 I just felt several ______________ of water fall on my head.

C Read the passage on page 22 again. Then, circle the correct answers.

1 Clouds are made of tiny drops of water and crystals of (hail / ice).

2 There are many different (types / styles) of clouds.

3 (Stratus / Cirrus) clouds are white clouds high in the sky.

4 Clouds at (low / medium) altitudes are alto clouds.

5 Stratus clouds (sometimes / always) indicate light rain.

D Read the passage. Then, use the words in the box to write the correct connecting words.

yet	for example	and	in addition

Many places around the world go through wet and dry periods. This means that it may rain a lot during some times of the year but might not rain at all during other months. When it rains a great deal, an area goes through its rainy season. During the rainy seasons in a few places, there may be periods when several centimeters of rain fall each day. ________________, in Asia, many regions get monsoons. Monsoons are seasonal changes in the winds. ________________, these changes also affect how much rain an area gets. Monsoon season in many countries in Asia happens during the summer. This is especially true in Southeast Asian countries such as Malaysia ________________ Thailand. Monsoon rains can benefit farmers greatly. ________________ they can also cause flooding and landslides in some places.

UNIT 04 Snow

A Read the passage on page 24 again. Then, write the answers to the questions.

1 What is snow?

____

2 When does water in clouds turn into ice crystals?

____

3 Where are some unusual places that snow falls?

____

4 How high may some snowdrifts be?

____

5 What can heavy snowfall do?

____

B Use the words in the box to complete the sentences. You may need to change the forms of the words.

snowdrift	Mother Nature	when it comes to	tropical paradise	power line

1 She spent her vacation in a ________________ in the South Pacific Ocean.

2 ________________ can be both beautiful and deadly.

3 ________________ making money, Jeff is better at it than most people.

4 There are some ________________ on the mountain that are several meters high.

5 The snowstorm caused many ________________ in the city to go down.

C Read the passage on page 26 again. Then, choose the correct answers.

1 Mark is on vacation in ________________.

a. Switzerland b. Austria c. France

2 A ________________ happened while Mark was mountain climbing.

a. rainstorm b. tornado c. blizzard

3 During the storm, Mark could only see ________________.

a. the sky b. white c. ice

4 Mark's guide told everyone not to ________________.

a. yell b. move c. run

5 Mark felt ________________ to return to his hotel.

a. lucky b. disappointed c. happy

D Read the passage. Then, circle the correct connecting words.

Snow is not the only form of frozen precipitation. Two other types are sleet and hail. There are a few differences between them. For instance, sleet usually falls during winter (because / while) hail typically falls during summer. Sleet falls to the ground as rain. (However / Therefore), as it falls, it encounters air that is below freezing. This causes the rain to turn into ice. (Before / When) it hits the ground, it is a combination of rain and frozen ice pellets. Hail, meanwhile, happens during thunderstorms. It falls as rain, (and / but) heavy winds cause the rain to move upward into cold air. This freezes the rain into ice pellets. (Since / As) it starts falling, it may be blown upward again. This can make the ice pellet to become very large. Most hail is the size of a pea. But some hail can be as large as a baseball.

C h a p t e r

2

Literature

UNIT

05 The Jungle Book

A **Read the passage on page 30 again. Then, write the answers to the questions.**

1 Where was Rudyard Kipling born?

____

2 When did Rudyard Kipling publish *The Jungle Book*?

____

3 Who are most of the stories in *The Jungle Book* about?

____

4 Who is Mowgli's greatest enemy?

____

5 What is the Law of the Jungle?

____

B **Use the words in the box to complete the sentences. You may need to change the forms of the words.**

abandoned	be centered upon	morals	reside	enemy

1 Shawn is a person of good ________________ who always behaves properly.

2 We are planning to ________________ in a large house in the countryside.

3 The house looks ________________, so no one probably lives there.

4 The book ________________ the actions of those two boys.

5 Eric and Brad are ________________ who dislike each other very much.

C Read the passage on page 32 again. Then, fill in the blanks with the correct words.

1 Rikki-Tikki-Tavi is the name of a ________________.

2 Rikki-Tikki-Tavi lives in ________________.

3 Two ________________ named Nag and Nagaina live near the house.

4 Rikki-Tikki-Tavi kills ________________ when he enters the house.

5 Rikki-Tikki-Tavi destroys all of the cobra ________________ in the underground lair.

D Read the passage. Then, choose where the sentence below best fits in the passage.

On popular story from *The Jungle Book* is "Kaa's Hunting." One day, several monkeys kidnap Mowgli. They take him to an abandoned city deep in the jungle. Baloo and Bagheera run after the monkeys. But they cannot keep up with the monkeys. They decide to get help from Kaa. Kaa is an enormous python. All of the monkeys are afraid of Kaa. Kaa agrees to help. So Baloo, Bagheera, and Kaa together go to the abandoned city. When Baloo and Bagheera arrive, the monkeys throw Mowgli into some ruins with cobras in it. But Mowgli convinces the cobras not to attack him. **A** Baloo and Bagheera fight the monkeys. **B** Kaa rescues Mowgli from the cobras. **C** Then, Kaa attacks the monkeys. **D** In the end, Baloo, Bagheera, and Kaa beat the monkeys. They rescue Mowgli, and they all return home safely.

But there are too many monkeys, so they start to lose.

UNIT 06 *Moby-Dick*

A Read the passage on page 34 again. Then, write the answers to the questions.

1 Where did Herman Melville sail?

____

2 What two books did Herman Melville write about his adventures on the ocean?

____

3 What is the first line of *Moby-Dick*?

____

4 Who is Captain Ahab?

____

5 What happens at the end of *Moby-Dick*?

____

B Use the words in the box to complete the sentences. You may need to change the forms of the words.

crew member	whaling ship	be narrated by	quest	tale

1 The knight is on a ______________ to kill a dragon and to save a princess.

2 Many ______________ spent two or three years on the ocean.

3 The story ______________ the author, who is the main character in the book.

4 In the past, people told ______________ out loud since few people knew how to read.

5 There are ten ______________ on board the ship now.

C Read the passage on page 36 again. Then, answer T (true) or F (false).

1 ______ The *Essex* was a whaling ship from Nantucket.

2 ______ There were twenty-one crew members on the *Essex*.

3 ______ A sperm whale two times the size of the *Essex* attacked the ship.

4 ______ Because of the whale, the *Essex* sank.

5 ______ Eight crew members died when the whale attacked the *Essex*.

D Read the passage. Then, choose where the sentence below best fits in the passage.

Like Herman Melville, Jack London wrote stories about animals. One of his most famous books is *The Call of the Wild*. It tells the story of Buck, a large dog that is kidnapped and taken to Alaska during the gold rush there. During his time in Alaska, Buck has to pull a sled with other dogs. He has several masters; some are good while others are bad. [A] Buck must deal with a number of problems during the story. [B] For instance, the weather is terrible. [C] In addition, there is a lot of violence, from other dogs and also from humans. [D] Finally, Buck gets a master that he loves. But his master is killed by Indians. In return, Buck attacks and kills many of the Indians. Then, he goes to live in the wild as he leads a wolf pack in the forest.

He also has to deal with dangers such as thin ice across rivers.

UNIT 07 William Shakespeare

A Read the passage on page 38 again. Then, write the answers to the questions.

1 Where was William Shakespeare from?

____

2 How many plays did William Shakespeare write?

____

3 What three genres are William Shakespeare's plays?

____

4 What is William Shakespeare's greatest comedy?

____

5 What is a sonnet?

____

B Use the words in the box to complete the sentences. You may need to change the forms of the words.

syllable	sonnet	be divided into	accomplished	role

1 A haiku is a Japanese poem that has seventeen ______________ in three lines.

2 Most plays ______________ three separate acts.

3 John Milton was an ______________ poet who wrote *Paradise Lost*.

4 Sam's ______________ in the play is Romeo, and Erica is going to be Juliet.

5 Shakespeare wrote many ______________, and some of them are very famous today.

C Read the passage on page 40 again. Then, circle the correct answers.

1 Christopher Marlowe was born in the same (month / year) as William Shakespeare.

2 Christopher Marlowe (never / quickly) became as famous as William Shakespeare.

3 Most of Christopher Marlowe's plays were (comedies / tragedies).

4 The play (*Dido* / *Tamburlaine the Great*) was about an emperor.

5 In *Doctor Faustus*, Faustus sells his (soul / mind) to the Devil.

D Read the passage. Then, use the words in the box to complete the classification charts.

Two of the greatest writers in the English language were Edmund Spenser and John Milton. Spenser lived from 1552 to 1599. He lived during the Renaissance in England. He is considered one of the greatest poets in the English language. His greatest work is *The Faerie Queene*. It is an epic poem that is divided into three books. Spenser wanted it to be longer, but he died before he could write more. John Milton also wrote poetry. Milton lived from 1608 to 1674. His greatest work was *Paradise Lost*. It tells the story of the fall of man in the Bible. Milton wrote the poem when he was blind. He dictated the lines to a person. Then, that person wrote them down. He also wrote *Paradise Regained* as well as other works of literature.

Paradise Lost | epic poem | blind | dictated | Renaissance | poets

Edmund Spenser

- Lived from 1552 to 1599
- Lived during the a. ______________
- Was one of the greatest b. ______________ in the English language
- Wrote *The Faerie Queene*
- Is an c. ______________

John Milton

- Lived from 1608 to 1674
- Greatest work was d. ______________
- Is about the fall of man
- Wrote the poem while he was e. ______________
- f. ______________ the lines
- Wrote *Paradise Regained* and other works

UNIT 08 Edgar Allan Poe

A Read the passage on page 42 again. Then, write the answers to the questions.

1 What types of writing did Edgar Allan Poe do?

____

2 What kinds of themes did most of Edgar Allan Poe's works have?

____

3 What is Edgar Allan Poe's best-known poem?

____

4 What genre were many of Edgar Allan Poe's short stories?

____

5 Who is C. Auguste Dupin?

____

B Use the words in the box to complete the sentences. You may need to change the forms of the words.

dark theme	be intended to	supernatural element	versatile	horror

1 This novel has a ________________ and focuses on death.

2 There is a ________________ in many myths from ancient cultures.

3 I enjoy reading ________________ stories even though they can be very frightening.

4 John is a ________________ actor who can perform many different kinds of roles.

5 This poem ________________ make readers think about love.

C Read the passage on page 44 again. Then, choose the correct answers.

1 C. Auguste Dupin was a ________________ in some short stories.

a. criminal b. detective c. police officer

2 C. Auguste Dupin appeared in Poe's work ________________.

a. *The Purloined Letter* b. *The Raven* c. *Annabel Lee*

3 *The Purloined Letter* tells about a letter that someone ________________.

a. stole b. copied c. wrote

4 C. Auguste Dupin has to get the letter back from a ________________ in the government.

a. secretary b. minister c. lady

5 The murderer in *The Murders in the Rue Morgue* is a(n) ________________.

a. sailor b. orangutan c. woman

D Read the passage. Then, complete the classification charts.

In the 1800s, many authors wrote horror stories. Two well-known horror stories were *Frankenstein* and *Dr. Jekyll and Mr. Hyde*. Mary Shelley wrote *Frankenstein* in 1818. It tells the story of Dr. Victor Frankenstein. He tries to create life from death. He succeeds, but he creates a monster that he is afraid of. The story tells about Frankenstein's rejection of the monster and the monster's attempts to get revenge on Frankenstein and his family. Robert Louis Stevenson wrote *Dr. Jekyll and Mr. Hyde* in 1886. It tells the story of Dr. Jekyll. He invents a potion that allows him to transform into Mr. Hyde. While Dr. Jekyll is a good man, Mr. Hyde is evil. The book shows the problems that can happen when a person does not control his bad side.

Frankenstein

- Was written by a. ________________ in 1818
- Is about Dr. Victor Frankenstein
- Creates b. ________________ from death
- Rejects the c. ________________
- Monster gets revenge on Frankenstein and his family

Dr. Jekyll and Mr. Hyde

- Was written by Robert Louis Stevenson in d. ________________
- Is the story of e. ________________
- Invents a potion
- Transforms into Mr. Hyde, an f. ________________ man

Chapter

3

Modern Technology

UNIT 09 Henry Ford and the Assembly Line

A Read the passage on page 48 again. Then, write the answers to the questions.

1 What did Henry Ford have a great effect on?

____

2 What company did Henry Ford found?

____

3 What was Henry Ford's goal?

____

4 Which of Henry Ford's cars was the most popular?

____

5 What was the new assembly method that Henry Ford installed?

____

B Use the words in the box to complete the sentences. You may need to change the forms of the words.

assembly method	demand	eventually	mass production	majority

1 There is a high ______________ for that popular smartphone these days.

2 ______________, I will come up with a good idea for a new project.

3 The company uses a unique ______________ to put together the computer chips.

4 A ______________ of the people in the city want their taxes to be lower.

5 The ______________ of many items has made their prices go down.

C Read the passage on page 50 again. Then, fill in the blanks with the correct words.

1 William Boeing owned a ________________ company before he became interested in airplanes.

2 William Boeing ________________ his airplane very much.

3 William Boeing founded his airline company in ________________.

4 After World War I ended, Boeing built ________________ aircraft.

5 Today, the Boeing Company is the world's largest ________________ company.

D Read the sentences and put them in the correct order. Then, rewrite the sentences by using the following words: *first*, *next*, *after that*, and *finally*.

1 ______ He established a steel company that became extremely successful.

2 ______ One of the greatest American industrialists was Andrew Carnegie.

3 ______ Carnegie began donating most of his fortune to charity and started establishing libraries and schools around the country.

4 ______ He got started in the railroad business.

5 ______ He sold his steel company for an enormous amount of money.

UNIT 10 Tim Berners-Lee and the World Wide Web

A Read the passage on page 52 again. Then, write the answers to the questions.

1 Which two countries were enemies in the 1960s?

____

2 What did ARPANET do?

____

3 When was the first email sent?

____

4 When did many people start to buy personal computers?

____

5 What did Tim Berners-Lee do?

____

B Use the words in the box to complete the sentences. You may need to change the forms of the words.

threat	have access to	share	version	personal computer

1 My father bought a ________________ for us to use at home.

2 There is a ________________ of war between those two countries.

3 What ________________ of that computer program are you using?

4 I am sorry, but I do not ________________ the information you need.

5 You ought to ________________ your knowledge with other people.

C Read the passage on page 54 again. Then, answer T (true) or F (false).

1 ______ Bill Gates is one of the richest men in the world.

2 ______ Bill Gates began programming computers when he was ten.

3 ______ Bill Gates graduated from Harvard in 1973.

4 ______ Bill Gates and Paul Allen started Microsoft together.

5 ______ Microsoft's software became popular in the 1970s.

D Read the sentences and put them in the correct order. Then, rewrite the sentences by using the words in the box.

after that	in 1976	in 1972	many years later	in the 1980s

1 ______ Steve Jobs went to Reed College, but he dropped out after one semester.

2 ______ Apple personal computers became very popular with many people.

3 ______ Apple sold the first iPod in 2001.

4 ______ Jobs and Steve Wozniak founded Apple Computer.

5 ______ In 2007, Apple began selling its first iPhone.

____

____

____

____

____

____

UNIT 11 Satellites

A **Read the passage on page 56 again. Then, write the answers to the questions.**

1 What was the name of the world's first artificial satellite?

____

2 About how many artificial satellites are currently orbiting the Earth?

____

3 What are the two kinds of satellites?

____

4 How does the modern telecommunications industry use satellites?

____

5 How do some militaries use satellites?

____

B **Use the words in the box to complete the sentences. You may need to change the forms of the words.**

Wi-Fi	artificial satellite	space agency	mobile phone	natural satellite

1 The ______________ is planning to send a mission to the moon next year.

2 You can use your ______________ to call people in most places in the country.

3 Jupiter has more than sixty ______________ orbiting it.

4 Thanks to ______________, we no longer need cables to connect to the Internet.

5 The rocket launched the ______________ and put it into orbit.

C Read the passage on page 58 again. Then, circle the correct answers.

1 Astronauts stayed in space for a few (days / weeks) in the early years of the Space Age.

2 People made (spaceships / space stations) to have a more permanent presence in space.

3 The Americans sent (*Almaz* / *Skylab*) into space in the 1970s.

4 The (Europeans / Soviets) sent the space station *Mir* into space.

5 There are currently (two / three) space stations orbiting Earth.

D Read the passage. Then, choose the correct summary sentence.

Most satellites stay in orbit around the Earth. But some of them go elsewhere in the solar system. Scientists want to learn about the sun, planets, and other objects in the solar system. So they have sent many satellites to explore them. These satellites are called space probes. The reason is that they conduct explorations of space. The first space probes went to the sun, Venus, and Mars. Later probes have visited the other planets in the solar system. Some have also flown by moons, comets, and asteroids. The most famous space probes are the *Voyager*, *Pioneer*, and *Mariner* series. Many more space probe missions are being planned. They will visit various places in the solar system. Thanks to all of the space probes that have been launched, we now know a great deal about the solar system.

a. Space agencies need to send more and more space probes throughout the solar system.
b. Space probes have provided humans with a lot of information about the solar system.
c. *The Voyager*, *Pioneer*, and *Mariner* space probes were the most successful satellites of all.

UNIT 12 The Industrial Revolution

A **Read the passage on page 60 again. Then, write the answers to the questions.**

1 When did people begin to invent a large number of machines?

____

2 Where did the Industrial Revolution begin?

____

3 Where did England get many raw materials from?

____

4 What was one of the most important inventions during the Industrial Revolution?

____

5 Which industries were affected by the Industrial Revolution?

____

B **Use the words in the box to complete the sentences. You may need to change the forms of the words.**

industrialize	countryside	raw material	be based on	grow crops

1 The ________________ in this region is beautiful, and few people live there.

2 Some important ________________ are wood, coal, and oil.

3 The economy of that country ________________ farming and mining.

4 The country is beginning to ________________, so it has many factories now.

5 That farmer ________________ such as wheat, barley, and corn in his fields.

C Read the passage on page 62 again. Then, choose the correct answers.

1 Ian and his brothers arrived in London ________________ ago.

a. one day b. one week c. one month

2 Ian and his brothers work at a ________________.

a. textile factory b. farm c. government agency

3 Ian's workplace is ________________ and not clean.

a. dark b. large c. old

4 Ian's parents live ________________.

a. in London b. abroad c. on a farm

5 The factories in London are always ________________.

a. expanding b. closing c. hiring

D Read the passage. Then, choose the correct summary sentence.

Around 1750, another revolution began in England. It was known as the Agricultural Revolution. During it, farmers in England became much more efficient and productive. There were several reasons for this. First, farmers began to plant different crops in their fields every year. This kept the soil from losing all of its nutrients. That way, many crops grew better in the soil. The farmers also took care when they were breeding their animals. So they made sure that only the biggest and strongest animals reproduced. They also began to use the machines that people were inventing. Thanks to these machines, farmers could plant large amounts of land. They could do that much faster than before, too. Thanks to the Agricultural Revolution, people in England were able to eat more food than ever before.

a. Famers in England produced more food than farmers in other countries.
b. The Industrial Revolution helped English farmers grow more crops than before.
c. There were three main reasons that the Agricultural Revolution happened.

Chapter

4

Economics

UNIT 13

The Silk Road

A Read the passage on page 66 again. Then, write the answers to the questions.

1 Which two ancient empires traded on the Silk Road?

____

2 Where did the Silk Road start?

____

3 How many major routes on the Silk Road were there?

____

4 What type of land did merchants have to cross on the Silk Road?

____

5 What did merchants trade on the Silk Road?

____

B Use the words in the box to complete the sentences. You may need to change the forms of the words.

wealthy	merchant	risk death	path	valley

1 Some people ________________ every day by doing jobs that are very dangerous.

2 The ________________ man lost a lot of his money when his ships sank.

3 The traders must cross the ________________ between the two mountains to get to the city.

4 There is a ________________ that you can take to get through the forest safely.

5 Many ________________ buy and sell goods in the market.

C Read the passage on page 68 again. Then, fill in the blanks with the correct words.

1 England had many colonies in ________________ in the 1600s and 1700s.

2 ________________ developed between England, Africa, and America.

3 Slaves were sent from ________________ to the American colonies.

4 The slaves worked on ________________ in America.

5 The American colonists sent many ________________ to England.

D Read the passage. Then, underline the causes and circle the effects.

In the 1400s, the Europeans wanted to trade for spices in Asia. But they could not go on the land route to Asia due to the Ottoman Empire. The Ottomans often fought with the Europeans. So it was too dangerous for them to go by land. They looked for sea routes instead. The Europeans tried to sail around Africa. It took them many attempts, but they finally managed to sail into the Indian Ocean. As a result, they could trade directly with people in Asia. Many Europeans sailed to India and other places in Asia. They traded for large amounts of spices such as pepper and cinnamon. Then, they sailed back to Europe and sold those goods. These sailors made a great amount of money in the spice trade. So many of them became very wealthy individuals.

UNIT

14 Bartering

A Read the passage on page 70 again. Then, write the answers to the questions.

1 What is bartering?

____

2 What does bartering not involve?

____

3 How long have people bartered?

____

4 Why might people who live far away from civilization barter?

____

5 Why might people in countries with poor economies barter?

____

B Use the words in the box to complete the sentences. You may need to change the forms of the words.

make a purchase	trade	value	currency	determine

1 What kind of _______________ do the people in China use?

2 If you would like to _______________, please speak with a salesman.

3 The _______________ of gold often rises during bad economic times.

4 We must _______________ how much these items are worth before we buy them.

5 I will _______________ these five books for your old bicycle.

C Read the passage on page 72 again. Then, answer T (true) or F (false).

1 ______ Many countries use paper bills and coins as money today.

2 ______ In the past, people used gold and silver coins as money.

3 ______ The Romans often paid their soldiers with pepper.

4 ______ Tulips were used as money in the Netherlands.

5 ______ Small rocks and shells were used as money in some cultures.

D Read the passage. Then, underline the causes and circle the effects.

In the 1590s, a trader brought some tulips to the Netherlands. The Dutch people thought the flowers were beautiful, so the value of tulips increased a great deal. Soon, many people began to sell tulips. Then, from 1634 to 1637, the tulip trade greatly increased. This was a period that many people called "tulip mania." The value of tulips grew dramatically. People could buy an entire house for a single tulip bulb. Suddenly, people realized that the tulip trade was out of control. Thus the prices of tulips dropped a great deal. There were some people who became wealthy from the tulip trade. But others lost almost all of their possessions. Since that time, tulips have remained valued flowers in the Netherlands. But they have never cost as much as they did from 1634 to 1637.

UNIT 15 Franchises

A Read the passage on page 74 again. Then, write the answers to the questions.

1 What does a franchise give a person the right to do?

____

2 What are the best-known kinds of franchises?

____

3 How does the company that owns the franchise help new owners?

____

4 When did franchises become popular?

____

5 What company helped make franchises very popular?

____

B Use the words in the box to complete the sentences. You may need to change the forms of the words.

look after	car dealership	support network	advantage	proven

1 Can you ______________ my dog while I am on vacation?

2 Tim has a ______________ of friends who help him during times of trouble.

3 That company has a ______________ record of success in its field.

4 Sarah bought a new vehicle from the big ______________ downtown.

5 Name three ______________ to going into business for yourself.

C Read the passage on page 76 again. Then, circle the correct answers.

1 The first McDonald's opened in (California / New York).

2 McDonald's used a food preparation system based on the (assembly line / steam engine).

3 Ray Kroc thought that McDonald's had a lot of (problems / potential).

4 Ray Kroc (bought / took) the rights to the restaurant from the McDonald brothers.

5 There are more than 34,000 McDonald's (factories / franchises) around the world today.

D Read the passage. Then, choose what them refers to.

Today, fast-food restaurants are some of the most popular franchises in the world. There are several reasons for this. First, they are able to cook and serve meals very quickly. Next, the meals that they serve are often inexpensive. This benefits the customers because they do not have to spend a great deal of money. The meals are often tasty, so people enjoy eating them. Finally, in recent years, fast-food restaurants have started to serve healthy meals. They still offer hamburgers, fried chicken, and pizza. Yet they also sell salads and other healthy alternatives. These new menu items have made the restaurants even more popular. As a result, there are tens of thousands of fast-food franchises all around the world. So they can be found in nearly every country on the planet.

a. the customers
b. the meals
c. people

UNIT 16 Changes in the U.S. Dollar

A Read the passage on page 78 again. Then, write the answers to the questions.

1 What type of money is used in the United States?

____

2 Where were the first dollars printed in America?

____

3 What did the colonist print for money before the war with England in the 1700s?

____

4 When were the first real American dollars printed?

____

5 Which three men's images have been on the ten-dollar bill?

____

B Use the words in the box to complete the sentences. You may need to change the forms of the words.

international	be accepted	print money	alteration	image

1 That country's money ________________ at the international bank.

2 There was an ________________ in the way that the dollar looked a few years ago.

3 Do you know which people's ________________ are on the money in your country?

4 You need a passport to take an ________________ trip.

5 The government is trying to ________________ to get itself out of debt.

C Read the passage on page 80 again. Then, choose the correct answers.

1 Julie thinks American money is ________________.

a. complex　　b. creative　　c. confusing

2 All American coins have different ________________.

a. shapes　　b. names　　c. sizes

3 A one-cent coin is called a ________________.

a. nickel　　b. penny　　c. dime

4 A ________________ is worth twenty-five cents.

a. dime　　b. nickel　　c. quarter

5 The coin with the greatest value is worth ________________.

a. twenty-five cents　　b. fifty cents　　c. one dollar

D Read the passage. Then, find the conjunctions and connecting words in the passage and circle them.

There are twenty-eight countries that belong to the European Union (EU) today. In the past, most of them had their own currency. For instance, the Germans used the mark. The French used the franc. And the Italians used the lira. However, today, the mark, franc, and lira no longer exist. In 1999, Germany, France, and Italy started to use the euro. They were not the only countries to use the euro though. Many other countries adopted it as well. Today, seventeen of the members of the EU use the euro. Not all of the members of the EU wanted to change to the euro. As an example, Great Britain did not adopt the euro. Instead, it kept the British pound. Poland, Sweden, and several other countries kept their own money as well.

Chapter 5

Ancient Societies

UNIT 17 Ancient Egypt

A Read the passage on page 84 again. Then, write the answers to the questions.

1 Where does the Nile River start and end?

____

2 When did people begin to farm the land around the Nile River?

____

3 When was ancient Egypt united under one kingdom?

____

4 Who were some great Egyptian pharaohs?

____

5 What did the Egyptians build all over their land?

____

B Use the words in the box to complete the sentences. You may need to change the forms of the words.

fertile	barren	monument	annual	thanks to

1 The land in this valley is ________________, so crops grow very well.

2 The ________________ dry season started, so it will not rain for a couple of months.

3 ________________ Mr. Sanderson, we finished the project on time.

4 The city built a ________________ to honor the man who founded it.

5 This desert is ________________, so nothing grows in it.

C Read the passage on page 86 again. Then, fill in the blanks with the correct words.

1 Many societies in ancient times grew up around ________________.

2 It was easy for people to ________________ goods on water.

3 ________________ means "the place between two rivers."

4 The Sumerian and ________________ empires formed in Mesopotamia.

5 The Sumerians had a form of government and their own ________________ system.

D Read the passage. Then, complete the outline by filling in the blanks.

Crete is an island in the eastern Mediterranean Sea. It is south of Greece and Turkey. And it is north of Egypt. Thousands of years ago, there was a great civilization there. It was called Minoan Civilization. Minoan Civilization started sometime around 3000 B.C. The capital was at Knossos. The palace of the king there had more than 1,500 rooms in it. Over time, the Minoans developed a very advanced civilization. They produced very good art. And they even had a written language. Unfortunately, around 1700 B.C., there was an earthquake in Crete. It destroyed many buildings. The Minoans rebuilt many of them. Then, around two centuries later, a volcano erupted near Crete. It sent a large tsunami that killed many people. After the tsunami, the Minoans disappeared.

Minoan Civilization

I. Was located in Crete
- i. Is south of Greece and Turkey
- ii. Is a. ________________ of Egypt

II. Started around 3000 B.C.

III. Had its capital at b. ________________
- i. King's palace had more than 1,500 rooms

IV. Developed an c. ________________ civilization
- i. Made good art
- ii. Had a d. ________________ language

V. Suffered disasters
- i. e. ________________ in 1700 B.C.
- ii. Tsunami two centuries later
- iii. Made the Minoans f. ________________

UNIT 18 The Chinese Qin Dynasty

A Read the passage on page 88 again. Then, write the answers to the questions.

1 Who unified China in 221 B.C.?

____

2 How important was the Qin Dynasty?

____

3 What did Qin Shi Huangdi try to standardize in China?

____

4 Who found Qin Shi Huangdi's tomb?

____

5 What was in Qin Shi Huangdi's tomb?

____

B Use the words in the box to complete the sentences. You may need to change the forms of the words.

tomb	founder	terracotta warrior	standardize	life-sized

1 The ______________ of the dynasty was one of the greatest kings in his country's history.

2 There are many ______________ statues in the art gallery.

3 No one knows where the ______________ of Genghis Khan is.

4 There are thousands of ______________ in Xian.

5 It will take a long time to ______________ the laws in the country.

C Read the passage on page 90 again. Then, answer T (true) or F (false).

1 ______ The writer was not impressed by the Great Wall of China.

2 ______ The Great Wall of China is one long wall.

3 ______ The Chinese started building the Great Wall around 2,500 years ago.

4 ______ The Great Wall is about 700 kilometers long.

5 ______ It took hundreds of years to build the Great Wall.

D Read the passage. Then, complete the outline by filling in the blanks.

The Mongol Temujin was born in 1162. He had a difficult life as a child because he was kicked out of his tribe. However, he trained hard and built up his own tribe. He started to conquer many Mongol tribes. Other tribes then made alliances with him. People started calling him "Genghis Khan." The name meant "great king." Genghis Khan decided to conquer lands outside Mongolia. First, he headed south into China. By 1215, he had captured Beijing and ruled much of China. Then, he took his armies west. His armies conquered land all throughout Asia and the Middle East. They even conquered much of Russia and part of Eastern Europe. By the time Genghis Khan died in 1227, he ruled the largest empire in the history of the world.

Genghis Khan

I. Was born in 1162
  i. Was named a. ______________
II. Built his own tribe and conquered other b. ______________ tribes
III. Started to be called "Genghis Khan"
  i. Means c."______________"
IV. Decided to conquer land outside Mongolia
  i. Captured d. ______________ and ruled much of China by 1215
  ii. Went e. ______________
  iii. Conquered land in Asia and the Middle East
  iv. Conquered land in Russia and Eastern Europe
V. Died in 1227
  i. Ruled the largest f. ______________ in world history

UNIT 19 Harappan Civilization

A **Read the passage on page 92 again. Then, write the answers to the questions.**

1 What happened to most human societies from the past?

____

2 Where was the Harappan Civilization?

____

3 What kind of culture did the Harappan people have?

____

4 What kind of writing system did the Harappan people use?

____

5 When did Harappan society end?

____

B **Use the words in the box to complete the sentences. You may need to change the forms of the words.**

without a trace	drought	fall	grid system	sewage system

1 The man went into the jungle and then vanished ______________.

2 This city was designed on a ______________, so it is easy to get around in.

3 Unless it rains soon, the ______________ is going to kill the crops in the fields.

4 The city ______________ when the attackers managed to break through the walls.

5 A problem with the ______________ is causing that awful smell.

C Read the passage on page 94 again. Then, circle the correct answers.

1 The Harappan people worshipped many (gods / angels).

2 The earliest known (story / writing) about Hinduism is the *Rig Veda*.

3 The *Rig Veda* was written down around (1000 B.C. / 300 B.C.)

4 Hinduism has many gods, so it is a (polytheistic / monotheistic) religion.

5 Vishnu and (Krishna / Shiva) were two of the most important Hindu gods.

D Read the passage. Then, look at the sentence below. Choose the answer choice that best simplifies the sentence.

For years, people thought that the Harappan Civilization was the oldest in India. Then, some divers in the Gulf of Cambay off western India made a shocking discovery. They found the ruins of an ancient city in water thirty-six meters deep. The city is around eight kilometers long. And it is almost four kilometers wide. Archaeologists have explored parts of this huge place. They have found parts of walls, sculptures, beads, and even human remains. When they dated these objects, they were surprised since the objects were more than 9,000 years old. That is 5,000 years older than any other known civilization in India. Archaeologists think the city existed at the end of the last ice age. When the weather got warmer, a lot of ice melted. This caused the water level to rise, so the city was covered with water.

When they dated these objects, they were surprised since the objects were more than 9,000 years old.

a. No one was surprised that some objects were 9,000 years old.
b. They were surprised that the items were over 9,000 years old.
c. None of the objects they found was less than 9,000 years old.

UNIT 20 The Aztec Empire

A Read the passage on page 96 again. Then, write the answers to the questions.

1 Where was Tenochtitlan built?

____

2 What kind of people were the Aztecs?

____

3 Why did many tribes living near the Aztecs fear them?

____

4 What did the Aztecs do during their religious ceremonies?

____

5 Who defeated the Aztecs?

____

B Use the words in the box to complete the sentences. You may need to change the forms of the words.

territory	settle down	human sacrifice	religious ceremony	power base

1 The empire continued to expand its ______________ by conquering new lands.

2 Many cultures performed ______________ in the past during various ceremonies.

3 The country's ______________ is its capital city, which is also a financial center.

4 We need to find a place to ______________ in and to call home.

5 Some cultures have unique ______________ that are interesting to watch.

C Read the passage on page 98 again. Then, choose the correct answers.

1 Alice is on vacation in ________________.

a. Mexico b. Honduras c. Guatemala

2 Chichen Itza used to be a large ________________ in Mayan times.

a. stadium b. palace c. city

3 The Mayan Empire was located in ________________ America.

a. North b. Central c. South

4 Mayan Civilization was great for around ________________ years.

a. 60 b. 600 c. 6,000

5 No one knows why Mayan society ________________.

a. collapsed b. formed c. changed

D Read the passage. Then, look at the sentence below. Choose the answer choice that best simplifies the sentence.

The three great empires of the Aztecs, Mayas, and Incas are well known. They were located in Central and South America. In North America, there was another great tribe of people. They were the Cherokees. They lived in the southeastern part of North America. The Cherokees lived in the area covered by the modern-day American states of Tennessee, Alabama, North Carolina, and others. They became a unique tribe around 1500 B.C. They lived in small independent city-states. The Cherokees had mostly friendly relationships with English colonists in the 1600s and 1700s. But, in the 1700s, more than half of the Cherokees died from a disease. After that, they began to become weaker as a tribe. They still exist though. Today, there are more than 300,000 members of the Cherokee Nation.

The Cherokees lived in the area covered by the modern-day American states of Tennessee, Alabama, North Carolina, and others.

a. The Cherokees were responsible for founding some American states.
b. Most Cherokees preferred to become residents of American states.
c. The Cherokees lived in places that are American states today.

memo

memo

We Bring You the World

Mastering Reading Skills Book 2

Mastering Reading Skills Book 2 has several objectives. First, it will help learners improve their English abilities, particularly their reading skills. Next, it will teach them valuable knowledge about a wide range of academic topics. The passages themselves will also entertain learners as they read. Finally, *Mastering Reading Skills Book 2* will help learners prepare for various standardized tests that they may take in the future. For instance, many questions about the passages are similar to those that appear on the iBT TOEFL® Junior and iBT TOEFL® exams. So, by using this book, learners should be able to get higher scores on the tests they take in the future.

For Basic-Level Readers

Developing Reading Skills Book 1
Developing Reading Skills Book 2

For Intermediate-Level Readers

Mastering Reading Skills Book 1
Mastering Reading Skills Book 2

Special Features

- **Academic and Entertaining Reading Passages**
  Contains 20 reading passages on all kinds of academic subjects
- **Reading Comprehension and Vocabulary Review Questions**
  Lets readers test their comprehension of the passages
- **Useful Reading Skills**
  Teaches readers important skills to make them better at reading
- **Detailed Word List**
  Provides definitions and sample sentences of difficult vocabulary words
- **Comprehensive Workbook**
  Contains extra questions, vocabulary exercises, and reading skill exercises
- **Recordings of Reading Passages**
  Lets readers improve their listening and pronunciation skills by listening to native speakers